RINALDO PILLA

Erotic Novus Ordo Seclorum

To the New World Order,

May future generations enjoy what we have tried to achieve for them, and their children.

Rinaldo Pilla, Venafro, 4th of July, 2013

After assumptions, accusations, and misunderstandings about the New World Order, "Erotic Novus Ordo Seclorum" aims to be a neutral analysis of this inevitable and upcoming era.

The School of Athens, Inc. is legally registered and effective with the Iowa Secretary of State since May 28, 2008, at 10:51 AM; Corporation number 36399 and U.S. Federal Employer Identification Number 26-2739417

Author Biography

Rinaldo Pilla was the founder of the modern School of Athens. A man of many trades; an imagist poet, humanist, philosopher, sculptor, entrepreneur, and man of science born about a century after Herman Hesse, only five years after the death of Ezra Pound, on the 24th of February 1977 in Turin, Italy. He was an artist of his kind, as well as a dedicated classic philanthropist, indisputable result of an intense Montessori and catechism educational method. His mother, Carmela Palumbo, was an art teacher born in a peasants' family at the time of World War II. His father, Luigi Pilla, was born and raised in Pozzuoli, near Naples, which is known in Southern Italy as Queen of the Bay.

At the age of sixteen, Rinaldo joined the prestigious Military Academy "Scuola Militare Nunziatella di Napoli," founded by Ferdinand IV of Bourbons in 1787, in a Jesuit fortress. There he finished his scientific high school studies, after which decided not to pursue the military life, and moved to Rome instead, to attend the European School of Economics. In 2001, there he gained a Bachelor of Arts Degree with Honors in International Business, by the Nottingham Trent University. During his undergraduate program, Rinaldo studied abroad at the University of Malta, which opened him a path to the New World.

In 2005, after a series of international living experiences, Rinaldo founded his first company, Pillawine Imports and later on, in May of 2008, he reopened the School of Athens, to bring back to life and to legality the ancient Academy. Plato originally founded the School of Athens in circa 387 BC in Athens, Greece, which persisted until 529 AD, when it was finally closed down by the Eastern Roman Emperor Justinian I. In 2006, he made his first air appearance as Aldo on PBS, American One Network, Clear Channel, CBS, NBC and HD Network with the New York based show, Taste This TV.

After a brief period in Des Moines, Iowa, he lived in Peoria, Illinois, before relocating back to Iowa, in Davenport. While in Peoria, Rinaldo attended the Illinois Central College, where he completed the Cisco Networking Academy, and later on became a CCNA. There, for distinguished academic achievements, Rinaldo also earned placement on the President's Honor List. At the Illinois Central

College, Rinaldo also attended a course to prepare for the Microsoft MCSE certification.

Rinaldo grew up in the town of Cicciano, in the province of Naples, until enlisting in the Nunziatella Military School. Cicciano is a small municipality contiguous with the towns of Cimitile and Nola. Cicciano was in part built by the Knights of Malta, at the time of the First Crusade. While, in antiquity, Cimitile was the necropolis (Latin for cemetery) of the town of Nola, and it was here that Saint Paulinus of Nola founded a monastic community.

The history of Cimitile is tied to its basilicas, whose principal nucleus developed around the II and III century AD. The municipality was originally called Coemeterium, for the presence of sepulchers and the tomb of Saint Felix. According to legend, the location was fruitful of miracles, and became an early destination of pilgrimages from every part of the Roman Empire. Near the end of the IV century, the basilicas complex achieved its maximum splendor, thanks to the bishop Pontius Meropius Anicius Paulinus, known as Saint Paulinus of Nola. He expanded the basilica of Saint Felix into the "basilica nova." He also introduced the first bell tower, and the Christian tradition and use of bells. Bells were invented to attract the masses and spread the oral message of the gospel among local populations well before the discovery and diffusion of the Books of the Bible.

Nola remained a municipium (Latin for municipality) with its own institutions and the use of the Oscan language until becoming a Roman colony, under Emperor Octavian Augustus, who died there on August 19, 14 AD, while visiting the place of his father's death. During the Second Punic War, from 218 to 201 BC, it thrice offered defiance to Hannibal in the first, second, and third Battle of Nola. In 73 BC Nola was stormed by Spartacus, and other seventy slaves, who fled to the caldera of Mount Vesuvius, near modern day Naples. For such a reason, Augustus and Vespasian established Roman colonies there. Nola is also Giordano Bruno's place of birth (1548-1600.)

Rinaldo was enrolled at Palmer College of Chiropractic in Davenport, Iowa from July 2005 until April 2008. He attended the Doctor of Chiropractic curriculum offered by the school, the first chiropractic college founded in the modern history of Western civilization. He was forced to suspend his studies after being arrested by the FBI, and the local SWAT team, on the 7th of April, 2008. Rinaldo was released from custody the day after, without explanations for his arrest. After about a year kept away from the campus facilities by the college itself, and many other several accidents with corrupt local police and the recruitment sergeants of the competent US Army recruitment station in Davenport, Rinaldo decided to relocate to Florida while working on his second book titled "The rise of Ba'al." However, he will move back to Italy instead, and teach English for Italian students in Nola.

Rinaldo's first book, "Proverbs, Poems and Economics of an American Immigrant" was completed in Davenport, which is renowned for being the birthplace of Leon Bismarck Beiderbecke, also known as Bix. He was an American jazz cornetist, composer, and pianist. Bix was born on March 10, 1903 and died on August 6, 1931 at the early age of only 28 years old. His fame though is recognized worldwide to the point that Italian movie directors Pupi and Antonio Avati decided to own Bix's birth house and early years' residence, on 1934 Grand Avenue, using it as their office in the USA. The poet and philosopher left his plants and a few personal belongings in that house before departing from Davenport to return to Italy.

Anyhow, by the end of 2010, the poet will move again to relocate to his mother's birth town of Venafro, in the Molise region of Southern Italy. Around the same period, Rinaldo collaborated with US writer and director Bill Still, author of "The Money Masters" and "The Secret of Oz," helping him with the translation of the script of The Secret of Oz into Italian. On the same topic, he also translated into English some of the Italian Prof. Giacinto Auriti's works on the legal nature of currency.

In 2012 the author gained a Master in Human Development & Learning (MHDL-1) by the University of Salerno, after having founded the Partito Libertario Italiano and the European Libertarian Party in Venafro, one year earlier in 2011. In fact, Rinaldo Pilla decided to run for Mayor of Venafro in the 2013 municipal elections. The year 2012 was a very proficient one for the poet, as he also made available for sale his book "Stato," in Italian, and his Master thesis titled "Samnite Semantics." With his thesis the author declared that its ambitious goal was not only to prove that Samnites belong to the tribe of Dan, but also to be nominated for a Nobel Prize in literature with such original work. The same year he also completed and published an erotic book titled "Pen Pals," in which he analyzes and exposes human sexuality through real dialogs with real members of the other sex.

Rinaldo slowly started to like Venafro, not only because he thought that Molise was the Land of Samson, but especially because of his acquaintances with the local political arena, which at first was not very kind, nor much willing to hear his proposals for the community, including the suggestion that Venafro should have twinned with Davenport. The same year he also applied for several job positions with the United Nations, in search of an income, while at the same time trying to restart his wine business from Italy.

The poet lived during the events of 9/11 and its consequences, under both George W. Bush presidencies, and was very critical of the President undertakings. However, later on Rinaldo clarified that the one thing he regretted having said in his book, "Proverbs, Poems and Economics," was Bush being the worst president in US history. Pilla realized that his administration may have strongly underestimated the overall network of infiltration and capability of the attackers, to the point it may have chosen not to disclose all details, particularly in regard of nano-thermite findings, to protect its already weakened public image.

By the end of 2012 Rinaldo's political campaign had gained more enemies than followers and supporters. So, Rinaldo figured the time for his views and proposals in Venafro wasn't right. During the same period, Rinaldo managed to register his US wine business in Italy as well, using a local notary in the near city of Isernia. Also, he send a copy of his Master thesis titles "Samnite Semantics" to Pope Benedict XVI, and received a correspondence from the Vatican letting him know that the gift had been delivered.

Few days before the new years' eve, Rinaldo wrote that looking back in prospective at his FBI arrest, he had come to realize it could have actually been very well legitimate, due to possible terrorist threats and money laundering screening and controls his international wine business activity may have required. Therefore, he could honestly say to have had a fair trial at the Scott County Jail and Courthouse. That was also meant to be a public apology to the Davenport Police, which was involved in his case, renewing them all his respect and gratefulness for their vigilance over him while living in Iowa.

After his relocation to Molise, Rinaldo got very interested in Samnite history. His studies continued even after the publication of his thesis, "Samnite Semantics," and later he declared to have reached the furthest possible explanation about the origin of his last name. In fact, it came to him as a big surprise when he learned that Pontius Pilate was in all actuality Samnite, even though a Roman citizen as well. Rinaldo deduced that the root of their last name was the same, "Pil-" and that the suffixes may have changed from "-ate" into "-la" over the course of history. The poet claimed he would have never known for sure if he had been Pilate's descendant. This however proved being a great explanation about the nature of his interest in the Holy Land.

The poet confessed that a cousin of his father living in Ercolano (from Latin Herculaneum) always used to say that the Pilla males were under a curse. Later on Rinaldo started to realize that she could have actually been referring to Galatians 3:10 or more in general to this possible link to Pontius Pilate. However, being himself of a Jewish haplotype, it would have made Pontius Pilate a Jew as well, and not only because he was Samnite. In a way or another, this would have implied that, no matter how, the Jews killed Christ. This would have also explained for the redundant fratricide theme, like Remus in classic Roman literature, which in this case opposed Pilate to Christ.

Nevertheless, the allegations about a possible blood lineage with Pontius Pilate made him reflect intensively about Pilate's role in the crucifixion of Christ. Rinaldo came to realize that Pilate did nothing more than God's willing by washing his hands off the matter. In fact, it was human weakness and corruption, not him that killed Christ. In addition, he thought this was also confirmed by the fact Pilate is venerated as a saint in Ethiopia. On the contrary, the version narrated by Nicolas Notovitch in "The unknown life of Jesus Christ," whereas Buddhist scripts report that Middle Eastern merchants accused Pilate to be responsible for Christ's death is biased. In fact, those were the same merchants and folks who betrayed Christ for gold, saving Barabbas.

In the end, the possibility of being Pilate's descendant was like a flashlight illuminating all of the author's previous intellectual and philosophical work. In fact, Rinaldo justified his great attraction and respect for blonde-haired and Nordic people, otherwise referred to as descendants of Yafet. In a way, he felt that unconsciously he had always known his real identity, and for such a reason he always felt an impulsive need to protect blonds from darkness, therefore his explanation of the Original Sin as intercourse between black men and white women. The idea that one of his ancestors may have actually known Christ and looked at Him in the eyes came to him as a message of true salvation by God, and forgiveness for Pilate's actions.

In order to provide even more evidence in support of his claim, Rinaldo suggested analyzing the significance of the Nativity as well. The three biblical Magi were a reference to the fact that Africa was already expecting the Messiah, which today is still confirmed by the veneration in Ethiopia of saint Pontius. Moreover, the star guiding the Magi was the North Star, as a reminder of Yafet people, therefore the importance for the descendants of Cam to respect their brothers and sisters, and especially avoiding again the original sin, which is washed away to everybody by mean of baptism. In fact, the descendants of Sam, i.e. Asian people, do not mix , but tend to marry among their closest similars.

In his opinion, Rinaldo also gave some important contribution to the English language, just as Shakespeare did. He used to explain that the origin of dual English alphabet style, which includes different spelling and phonetic components, derived directly from Caesar's cipher. In fact, Caesar invented a ciphered Latin alphabet to communicate securely with his officials, eluding possible interceptions of his messages by Northern tribes. However, soon after the Celts figured it out, and assimilated Caesar's strategy in their own language in order to elude the Romans. Therefore, Caesar was one of the fathers of the English language.

Also pretty original was Rinaldo's own explanation of Pilate's inscription I.N.R.I. during the crucifixion. According to the author, scholars had focused too much on the gesture of Pilate washing his hands, and too little on what he actually did. It is possible that Rome knew about the Samnites' origin and link to Israel, therefore it was not by chance that Pontius was chosen as Roman procurator to Judea. Pilate may have decided to write "Iesus Nazarenus Rex Iudaeorum," meaning Jesus, King of the Jews as to recognize him as the Lord, and not to offend the Jews. That might have been the only thing he was capable of doing, in order to pass it onto history in his own words.

As a matter of fact, both Nola and Cimitile were Samnite territories as well, and Pilate may have been the first person to ever convert to Christianity in human history. This would explain the presence of the first bell tower in Cimitile, as well as the first oral teachings of the Gospel. This would also make Samnites the very first Christians in general. Furthermore, this would make the Roman villa in Venafro, "Pilate's villa," and Rinaldo even suggested that his tomb could be in the grotto behind Venafro's Pandone Castle or under the Cathedral. That however was just his marketing campaign for the City of Venafro knowing very well his thesis could not be proven, nor the obvious fact he was not a descendant of Pilate. Nevertheless, Rinaldo always declared being a bit of a poet. In a way, that was also a good teaching lesson on how dictators can easily use history to create myths against the masses to enslave them.

In order to bring even more evidence to his thesis, Rinaldo also suggested that Mount Holy Cross in Venafro was an ancient stone quarry, whereas Samnites first, then Romans started to extract bare stone from the peak summit, letting it roll down the slope all the way to the valley. Once down the hill, stonemasons would have carved the stones into columns and anything else. Finally, in 2013 Rinaldo decided to retire to private life, hoping to make some bucks as an entrepreneur and questioning atheism after concluding that Villa Pilato in Venafro might have been just a counterfeit. Rinaldo also thanked all the people who, in a way or another, helped him write his books, and to realize that pedophilia is the forbidden fruit, whereas the origin of all-evil. He also publically admitted having a bit of a rebel demeanor, especially when criticizing the political arena.

Pilla's explanation of the original sin was also very peculiar. In his own words, the snake was a reference to paganism in general, as represented by the voodoo god Damballah, which is represented by a snake as well. The symbolic use of the voodoo snake also supported a deeper, hidden interracial sexual message, which the poet never felt ashamed of addressing. For the records, Pilla also wanted everyone to know his writings aimed to be the proof he did not commit any misdemeanors while living in the US, which is what really mattered to him most.

Contents:

Nonostante il Parco Nazionale della Momoria Storica di San Pietro Infine, al 2013 c'è ancora chi pensa che le bandiere siano solo stracci per pulircisi il culo.

Despite the National Memorial Park of San Pietro Infine, in 2013, there are still people who think that flags are only rags to clean their ass with.

Chi non ha memoria è senza futuro e questo è il vero ed unico messaggio della locuzione latina: "errare humanum est, perseverare autem diabolicum"

Who has no memory has no future, and that is the real and only meaning of the Latin phrase: "errare humanum est, perseverare autem diabolicum."

Il Nuovo Ordine Mondiale altro non è se non il trionfo della legalità e della giustizia, a meno che ciò non sia quel che i cittadini desiderino, per altri non ben chiari ed oscuri motivi.

The New World Order is nothing more than the triumph of law and justice, unless this is not what citizens want, for other unclear and obscure reasons.

Senza il più assoluto rispetto della legalità non vi potrà mai esser pace ed è altrettanto semplice capire chi benefici della guerra, della lotta e del contrasto all'illegalità.

Without the most absolute respect of legality, there can never be peace, and it is equally simple to understand who benefits of wars and illegality.

La spada "Gladio" rappresenta il massimo della tecnologia militare dell'antica Roma.

The sword "Gladius" represents the summit of ancient Rome's military technology.

Buona Pasqua a tutti dal "MURO INRI".

Happy Easter everybody from the "INRI WALL." (Mar 31, 2013)

Oggi più che mai è importante ricordare anche quanto vitale sia per il mondo la conoscenza di tutte le religioni in Terra, da cui deriva l'ecumenismo, affinché queste possano dialogare e non solo attraverso i propri sacerdoti, ma soprattutto tra persone comuni che possano facilitare la pace tra gli uomini.

Today, more than ever, it is important also to remember how vital it is for the world to know all religions on Earth. This is the essence of ecumenism, so religions can communicate with each other, and not only through their own priests or clergy representatives, but especially among ordinary people, who can accelerate the peace process among humans.

Il fanatismo religioso è il carburante dell'odio tra gli uomini ed alla base di ogni conflitto, sebbene già a seguito della Seconda Guerra Mondiale tutte le Nazioni si impegnarono a far in modo che la tolleranza guidasse le coscienze di tutti, sottoscrivendo la Dichiarazione universale dei diritti umani. Purtroppo, ancora oggi tale documento viene ignorato e dismesso, a fronte di convinzioni proprie ideologiche e religiose.

Religious fanaticism is the fuel of hatred among men, and the fountainhead behind every conflict. This is still true; despite in the aftermath of the Second World War, all nations committed themselves to ensure that tolerance would guide the consciences of them all, undersigning to the Universal Declaration of Human Rights. Unfortunately, even today such document is ignored and dismissed, in front of ideological and religious beliefs.

Ancor oggi, le varie religioni si fanno concorrenza come se fossero in guerra e solo per accaparrarsi il bottino.

Even today, the various religions compete as if they were at war, and only to grab the loot.

Letteralmente, sono ormai diversi anni che scrivo. I miei interessi hanno spaziato attraverso tutte le materie della conoscenza umana, ciò nonostante abbia impiegato maggior parte delle mie energie sull'economia globale e commercio internazionale. Molto spesso, quello che via via imparavo mi disturbava fortemente, causando grandi critiche verso le autorità e le istituzioni. A causa dei segreti professionali, quali bancari, legali e segreti di stato, non è stato facile ricercare la verità. Lentamente, tuttavia, sono giunto alla conclusione che la maggior parte delle preoccupazioni e critiche popolari contro i governi occidentali sono solo una sciocchezza. Sono contento di aver avuto modo di rendermene conto, nonostante mi ci siano voluti anni di studi, ricerche e chilometri d'inchiostro.

Literally, I have been writing for several years now. My interests have varied across all subjects of human knowledge; despite I have focused most energy on the global economy and international business. Very often, what I was learning about strongly disturbed me, causing great criticism towards authorities and institutions. Because of professional secrets, such as bank, legal and State secrets, studying for truth was not easy. Slowly however, I got to the conclusions that most of the popular concerns and critiques against Western governments are just nonsense. I am glad I got to realize this; despite it took years of studying, researching, and eventually writing.

Dopotutto Einstein non aveva tutti i tori a professarsi ateo. L'ateismo è di gran lunga più salutare per la psiche umana di qualsiasi altra religione, sebbene associato al comunismo potrebbe divenire un'arma letale.

After all, Einstein was not that wrong professing himself atheist. Atheism is far healthier for the human mind than any other religion. Although, associated with communism, could become a lethal weapon.

Non mi rimane che fare il pornostar per raccimolare qualche quattrino.

To make a few bucks, I can only try becoming a porn star.

Le donne mafiose sono come mantidi religiose.

Mafia women are like praying mantises.

Un grazie agli "Zengars" di Venafro, per la loro demenza, senile e non, omertà, i clacson e lo sbattare porte, cancelli e battiscopa che m'è stato di gran ispirazione!

Thanks to the "Zengars" of Venafro, for their dementia, senile and not, omertà, their honking, the slamming of doors, gates and baseboards, as it was of great inspiration!

Gran parte degli edifici civili italiani al 2013, per lo più edificati nel dopoguerra con strutture portanti in cemento armato, necessita interventi di consolidamento. Ciò è dovuto maggiormente al naturale deterioramento del ferro utilizzato nell'armatura del cemento, che in sé è resistentissimo alla forze comprimenti, ma fragilissimo alla flessione. Tale pecca del cemento fu ovviata appunto mediante l'armatura in ferro, per aggiungere al cemento la necessaria resistenza alla flessione. Dopo settant'anni, è tempo di cominciare a prevenire ulteriori indebolimenti delle strutture, soprattutto a causa della natura geologica del suolo italiano, sospeso tra la faglia terrestre euroasiatica ed africana, quindi a grande rischio sismico. Gli interventi dovrebbero essere mirati a sostituire con nuovi materiali la capacità del cemento, come ad esempio utilizzando rinforzi di fibra di carbonio, anche per i solai, che dovrebbero inoltre essere insonorizzati per evitare l'escalare di liti condominiali dovute agli "Zengars" che potrebbero di proposito e non accidentalemnte sbattere le scope sui battiscopa, tormentando i propri vicini. Inoltre, gli edifici vanno anche isolati termicamente, come richiesto dalle più recenti normative europee in materia. Lo stesso discorso vale per i palazzi storici italiani, che ormai dovranno essere consolidati alla stessa maniera, per evitare che vengano del tutto persi come a l'Aquila e Ferrara. La riluttanza del popolo verso tali interventi, che richiedono putroppo a volte la modifica dell'aspetto estetico di tale patrimonio artistico ed architettonico non può essere presa più in alcuna considerazione datosi i risultati dei più recenti danni sismici sopraindicati e che hanno gravente intaccato le già pessime condizioni economiche del Bel Paese.

Most of the Italian civil buildings, as of the year 2013, which were built in the postwar period, using reinforced concrete structures, require consolidation operations. This is due mostly to the natural deterioration of steel used in reinforcing the mortar, which in itself is highly resistant to compressive forces, but fragile to flexion or tensile ones. This issue was resolved using steel armors, to add to concrete the required flexural strength. After 70 years, it's now time to begin preventing further weakening of the structures, mainly because of the geological nature of the Italian ground, suspended between the Eurasian and African Earth fault, therefore at high seismic risk. Interventions should be targeted to replace cement capacity with new materials, such as using carbon fibers reinforcements, including floors or ceilings, which should also be soundproofed to avoid an increase of communal quarrels, due to the "Zengars," who may purposely, not accidentally, torment their neighbors by banging brooms on baseboards. In addition, the buildings should be thermically insulated as well, as required by the latest European standards and regulations. The same goes for Italian historical buildings, which must be consolidated the same way, to prevent them from being completely lost, as in the case of L'Aquila and Ferrara. The reluctance of people to such interventions, which unfortunately may sometimes require the changing in the appearance of the Italian artistic and architectural heritage, can no longer be taken into consideration, after the results of the latest seismic damages indicated above, which have also affected the already poor economic conditions of the "Bel Paese."

Il Colosseo andrebbe dato in gestione ai finlandesi, come hanno chiesto.

The Coliseum should be given to the Finnish for management, as requested.

Il Parco della Memoria Storica di San Pietro Infine necessita urgentissimi interventi di consolidamento.

The WWII Memorial Park of San Pietro Infine, as of today, Apr 2, 2013, needs consolidation operations very urgently.

Per il suo patrimonio storico-culturale, Venafro andrebbe dichiarata patrimonio dell'umanità e quindi aggiungersi alla lista dei siti UNESCO, ma soprattutto per evitare che i venafrani facciano marcire tutto.

Due to its cultural and historical heritage, Venafro should be declared a World Heritage Site, i.e. be added the list of UNESCO sites, but especially to prevent its inhabitants from letting everything go rotten.

Ieri, 31/3/2013, si sono notate feci di lupo nei pressi della Torretta Normanna di Venafro. Ciò è indice del fatto che ad alta quota il cibo stia cominciando a scarseggiare per gli animali, per tanto hanno cominciato a cercare da mangiare più in giù. La noncuranza degli abitanti locali e l'impatto dell'uomo in genere sull'ecosistema, a partire dal riscaldamento globale è da ritenersi responsabile per lo sconvolgimento dei naturali equilibri della biosfera. Purtroppo la popolazione non risponde affatto alle campagne di sensibilazzione sia internazionali, da parte delle Nazioni Unite, sia nazionali da parte del Governo. Infatti, invana sarà pure quest'ennesima annotazione.

Yesterday, 3/31/2013, I have noticed some wolf stools by the Norman Tower of Venafro. This is an indication of the fact that high-altitude food is beginning to run low for the animals, therefore they have began looking for food at lower altitudes. The neglect of the local inhabitants, and the overall human impact on the ecosystem in general, causing global warming, is responsible for the disruption of the natural balance of the biosphere. Unfortunately, the population does not respond at any international awareness campaigns, by the United Nations, nor national ones, by the Italian Government. In fact, most likely, this nth annotation of mine will also be unnoticed and ignored, and by the local Italian WWF as well, which I am a member of.

Di certo non voglio fare la stessa fine di Leopoldo Pilla.

Certainly I don't want to end up like Leopoldo Pilla.

Non posso essere il Messia, figlio di Giuseppe, in quanto non appartengo alla Casa di Giuseppe né quella di Davide, bensì a quella di Dan, per mezzo di Sansone, essendo di origini sannite.

I cannot be the Messiah, son of Joseph, as I do not belong to the House of Joseph or David, but to the Tribe of Dan, by mean of Samson, being of Samnite origins.

Gli "Zengars" di Venafro sembrano non capire cosa sia il divieto di segnalazione acustica entro i limiti urbani e tantomeno i vigili che ignorano le infrazioni degli abitanti come se Venafro fosse ferma ai tempi del Far West.

The "Zengars" of Venafro seem not to understand what a ban on honking within urban limits is, as well the local patrol, which ignores those who commit the infringements, as if Venafro was frozen in history at the time of the Wild West.

L'ecunemismo non può non avere alla base i dieci comandamenti dati a Mosè da Dio.

Ecumenism cannot but be based upon the Ten Commandments given to Moses by God.

Il segreto del culturismo è quello di fare del culto altrui la propria forza, proprio come insegna il Judo, sebbene l'intento di quest'ultimo non sia quello di diventare grossi e fessi, ma snelli ed efficaci.

The secret of bodybuilding is to make of others' worshipping your strength, just like Judo teaches, although the latter's intent is not to become big and dumb, but lean and effective.

"Mens sana in corpore sano" significa essere proprio come la spada romana "Gladio". Non è la forza del soldato a farla muovere, bensì il suo perfetto bilanciamento, frutto del più raffinato studio, applicato al più arduo addestramento.

"Mens sana in corpore sano" means to be just like the Roman sword "Gladio." It is not the strength of the soldier to make it move, but its perfect balance, result of the most refined study, applied to the hardest training.

Anche l'arte del buon barbiere si può dire abbia una forte impronta sannita, in quanto Sansone fu beffato da Dalila, che lo vendette per quattro soldi, proprio come Eva fece ad Adamo. Da allora, meglio farsi tagliare i capelli da un barbiere che da una parrucchiera. Ovviamente questo vale solo per i maschi sanniti.

The art of a good barber can be said to have a strong Samnite origin as well, as Samson was mocked by Dalila, who sold him out for four pennies, just like Eve did to Adam. Since then, it's better to get a hair cut by a barber, rather than a hairdresser. Of course, this only applies to Samnite males.

L'Unione Europea non è altro che la versione moderna della storia dell'antica Roma. Infatti, l'elite delle popolazioni italiche pre-romane, come sanniti, greci, messapi, apuli, sardi, umbri, etruschi, sabini, latini ed infine celti decisero di dare alla penisola italica un nuovo ordine per meglio gestire i territori e così è per l'UE. Roma fu di fatto frutto di un accordo tra tutte queste "Nazioni" a riorganizzarsi in unico Stato e la decisione non fu accettata dalle classi sociali più basse delle tribù, al punto che ci vollero le guerre civili affinché Roma imponesse il suo dominio. Si spera l'Europa ci riesca senza ripetere tali eventi. Ad ogni modo, la stessa storia è già riuscita con successo negli Stati Uniti d'America. Ciò implica che la storia di Roma sia la storia del mondo, quindi l'espressione "Caput Mundi".

The European Union is just a modern version of Rome's ancient history. In fact, as the elite of Italy's main populations before Rome, such as Samnites, Greeks, Messapians, Apulians, Sardinians, Umbrians, Etruscans, Sabines, Latins, and finally Celts decided to give the Italian peninsula a new order to better manage their territories, so is the case for the EU. Rome was basically the result of an agreement among all these "Nations" to reorganize them under one State, and the decision was not accepted among the lower classes of all tribes, to the point it took the civil wars for Rome to impose its domain. Hopefully Europe will succeed avoiding such repetition of events. By the way, the same story already successfully happened in the United States of America. This means that the history of Rome really is the history of the world, therefore the expression "Caput Mundi."

Dopotutto il Nuovo Ordine Mondiale non è affatto così nuovo come si può pensare.

After all, the New World Order is not at all as new of a concept as one may think.

Un'ulteriore evidenza che i Sanniti appartenessero alla tribù di Dan viene dalle testimonianze della dominanza longobarda del territorio sannita, noto all'epoca come Ducato di Benevento. I longobardi provenivano dalla Danimarca e quindi i sanniti sarebbero in realtà "danniti", ossia provenienti da Dan, sebbene a specificarne ulteriolmente la vera identità è proprio San, ossia Sansone, anch'egli appartenente alla tribù di Dan.

Further evidence that the Samnites belonged to the tribe of Dan comes from the testimonies of Lombard dominance of the Samnite territory, known at the time as the Duchy of Benevento. The Lombards were from Denmark, therefore Samnites would actually be "dannites," coming from Dan, despite further specification regarding their true identity is given by Sam, i.e. Samson, also belonging to the tribe of Dan.

Il simbolo della Tribù di Dan è il simbolo del mosaico di Villa Pilato a Venafro. Dan significa "giudice", proprio come Ponzio Pilato.

The symbol of the tribe of Dan is represented by the mosaic at Villa Pilate in Venafro. Dan means "judge," just like Pontius Pilate.

I venafrani hanno fatto di tutto per interferire, ostacolare ed intralciare i miei studi sin da quando mi ci sono trasferito.

The inhabitants of Venafro have done everything to interfere, obstacle and disrupt my studies, since I have moved here.

Nella vita ho scelto di studiare, non di zappare e non perché ritenessi il lavoro nei campi indegno delle mie attenzioni.

In life I have chosen to study, not hoeing, and not because I felt the work in the fields as unworthy of my attentions.

Nella storia dell'antica Roma è possibile dire che Giulio Cesare rappresenti un colpo di stato vero e proprio o quantomeno la persona che ha segnato volontariamente o meno la transizione da Repubblica a Impero. Ciò è ulteriolmente supportato dalla scelta di Virgilio di narrare in forma epica le origini di Roma e della dinastia Iulia che altrimenti non avrebbe trovato alcun riscontro con le tradizioni della leggenda della fondazione di Roma, per mezzo dei suoi Sette Re, che non seguivano affatto una linea familiare o etnica ben precisa, ma erano meglio rappresentativi dell'accordo tra le popolazioni italiche pre-romane a governarsi secondo un nuovo ordine, che per l'appunto diede vita alla Repubblica, ossia all'SPQR.

In the history of ancient Rome, one could say that the persona of Julius Caesar represents a coup itself, or at least the person who, willingly or not, marked the transition from Republic to Empire. Besides, this is also supported by the choice of Virgil to narrate in epic form the origins of Rome, as well as the Julia dynasty. In fact, it wouldn't have been possible otherwise to legitimate their ruling rights, according to the oral traditions of the legend of the founding of Rome, by means of its Seven Kings, who were not at all chosen by familial line or specific ethnic origins. On the contrary, they were better representative of the agreement between the italic pre-Roman peoples to govern themselves in accordance with a new order, which in fact gave birth to the Republic known as SPQR.

Non comprendo la riluttanza dei senza fissa dimora a rivolgersi alle strutture ad essi predisposte anzicché dedicarsi all'accattonaggio per strada.

I do not understand the reluctance of the homeless to find shelter at the proper facilities appointed just for them, instead of begging on the street.

Non voglio che le generazioni future pensino abbia cambiato idea all'improvviso nei miei scritti, bensì considerino solo le conclusioni cui sono giunto dopo i miei lunghi studi.

I don't want future generations to think I suddenly changed my mind in my writings, but only consider the conclusions I got to, after my long studying.

Non comprendo come l'adozione non venga considerata quale naturale alternativa all'aborto e soprattutto nel miglior interesse dei minori quando i genitori giacciono in condizioni economiche avverse per la propria incolumità tanto quanto dei propri figli.

I do not understand how adoption is not considered the natural alternative to abortion and, above all, in the best interest of minors when parents lie in adverse economic conditions for their own safety as much as their children.

Dopo il disordine, il mondo cerca di tornare al suo normale ordine ed equilibrio spontaneamente.

After chaos, the world tries to return to its normal order and balance spontaneously.

I dialetti italiani sono lingue barbare, risultato dell'isolazionismo.

Italian dialects are barbarous language, result of isolationism.

La cultura mafiosa e l'omertà sono il risultato dell'isolazionismo.

The mafia code of silence and culture are the result of isolationism.

Le culture mafiose o terroristiche rifiutano il Nuovo Ordine Mondiale in quanto gli è troppo scomodo.

The mafia or terrorist culture reject the New World Order because it is too awkward for their occult interests.

La cultura mafiosa o terroristica si oppone all'educazione in quanto solo al buio ed allo scuro può operare indisturbata.

The mafia or terrorist culture opposes education because it can operate unhindered only hidden in the dark.

L'ignoranza altro non è che malnutrizione mentale. Sebbene a differenza della fame fisica, essa sia ingiustificabile a cospetto della Legge.

Ignorance is nothing more than mental malnutrition. Although, unlike physical hunger, it is unjustifiable in front of the Law.

Given that denying God's existence or even a creator in general is equal to denying one's own existence, this implies a person who does not recognize himself or herself as belonging to creation itself. This "forma mentis" is similar to that of men before Galileo, when man thought to be at the center of the universe, rather than on a rotating ball, freely gravitating and suspended in space. On one hand, denying a creator signifies egocentrism, while on the other, full and unquestioned submission to a creator signifies nullity. Despite the undeniable right to free will and own thoughts and ideas, the modern balanced mind cannot ignore the statement given by René Descartes, "Dubito, ergo cogito, ergo sum." In English this translates as, "I doubt, therefore I think, therefore I am." The answer to the archaic question of who we really are does not seem to have found any final arrival yet. However, neither atheism, i.e. the rejection of God, nor obsessive faith have proven able to improve the quest or the human conditions in general along the way. One can even speculate that we perceive existence only through our thoughts, therefore thought is our only connection to God, which we are constantly trying to improve, in order to reach this entity. In a way, we only seem to be evolving in order to allow for our own thoughts to evolve and refine. Will we ever be able to meet God? It does not really matter, as the more we travel in space and time, the better our lives on Earth become. Denying the evidence is diabolic, as much as denying man's own existence. In media stat virtus, i.e. balance is to be found half way, as for all things which are contained in the universe as we can perceive it, as creation or not.

In principio era la Parola o Verbo, che comunque è una parola, ma gli "Zengars" invece con la loro omertà hanno scelto di rimanere col mondo animale, muti e finti tonti.

In the beginning was the word or verb, which nevertheless is a word, but the "Zengars," with their silence, have chosen to stay with the animal world, dumb.

Si può dire che Cristo sia stato la prima tra le vittime dell'omertà, tant'è vero che se non fosse stato per la Bibbia e le tradizioni orali diffuse da Ponzio Pilato di ritorno dalla Giudea, di Lui non si saprebbe nulla, in quanto gli storici ufficiali di Roma hanno fatto di tutto per cancellarne ogni traccia.

It is possible to say that Christ was the very first victim of the code of silence known as omertà. Had it not been for the Bible, and the oral tradition spread by Pontius Pilate after his return from Judea, He would have gone unnoticed, as Rome's official historians did everything to erase any references of Him.

Il Nuovo Ordine Mondiale è l'unica soluzione per la pace in Terra.

The New World Order is the only possibility for peace on Earth.

Con l'inizio di primavera e l'arrivo delle mosche, oltre alla venere mangiamosche è importante sapere che le lucertole se ne nutrono, per cui è fondamentale non disturbarle e non temerle.

With the beginning of spring and the arrival of flies, in addition to the Venus flytrap, it is important to know that lizards also eat them, so it is fundamental not to disturb or fear the reptiles.

Per il loro ossessivo attaccamento al passato, alle origini ed alle cattive abitudini, gli "Zengars" troveranno i cancelli chiusi per il futuro.

For their obsessive attachment to the past, their origins and bad habits, the "Zengars" will find the gates closed for the future.

Gli "Zengars" non sono in grado di chiudere porte e cancellate senza sbatterle, in quanto essi inconsciamente pensano di vivere in stalle per il bestiame, per il cui i loro vicini o il prossimo in genere non hanno alcuna importanza, conta solo spacciarsi per bestia più molesta.

The "Zengars" are reluctant to closing doors and gates without whisking them, because subconsciously they think to be living in a pigsty, therefore their neighbors have no importance, but only appearing as the noisiest beast matters.

Il modello ideale cui gli "Zengars" si rifanno ed aspirano è la bestia 666.

The ideal model the "Zengars" relate to and aspire is the beast 666.

Al 2013 gli "Zengars" credono ancora alla magia e alla superstizione anzicché alla scienza.

As of 2013, the "Zengars" still believe in magic and superstition rather than science.

Come io ho scelto un nominativo ed un'identità fittizia, quale "Zengars", per indicare gli adepti delle sette di mafia, camorra, 'ndrangheta e sacra corona unita, così è lecito pensare fecero gli autori antichi con la mitologia.

As I have chosen a fictitious name and identity, such as "Zengars," to indicate the sect adepts of mafia, camorra, ' ndrangheta and sacra corona unita, so ancient writers may have done with mythology.

Il Nuovo Ordine Mondiale è stanco dei continui corsi e ricorsi storici.

The New World Order is tired of history constantly repeating.

Chi tace acconsente, per cui gli omertosi sono complici e colpevoli tanto quanto i mafiosi.

Who is silent gives consent, therefore is accomplice and guilty as much as the gang members.

La parola mafia deriva dall'arabo "maha^", ossia grotta per indicarne l'origine ed il modus operandi occulto e nascosto, come i ratti nelle fogne. (^ Gambetta, The Sicilian Mafia. pp. 259-261.)

The word mafia comes from the Arabic "maha^," as to indicate its occult and hidden origin and modus operandi, like rats in the sewers. (^ Gambetta, The Sicilian Mafia. pp. 259-261.)

Senza mezzi termini, la Terza Guerra Mondiale per l'Italia sarà la guerra per debellare la mafia, ossia il terrorismo interno, con tutti i suoi tentacoli internazionali.

Bluntly, the Third World War for Italy will be the war to eradicate mafia, namely domestic terrorism, with all of its international tentacles.

Gli "Zengars" non comprendono che in una Repubblica non contano i numeri ma solo e soltanto i diritti dell'individuo. Infatti, non mi stancherò mai di dirlo, in una semplice democrazia, due lupi ed un agnello potrebbero votare di mangiarsi l'agnello. In una Repubblica ciò non è possibile, benché i lupi abbiano di fatto i 2/3 della maggioranza elettorale.

The "Zengars" do not seem to understand that in a Republic numbers do not count, but only the rights of the individual do. In fact, I'll never tire of telling that, in a simple democracy, two wolves and a lamb could vote to gobble up the lamb. In a Republic, that is not possible, despite the wolves have the 2/3 of the electoral majority.

Sempre meglio vendersi al Nuovo Ordine Mondiale che essere venduti all'uomo nero da una madre ignorante.

It's always better to give oneself out to the New World Order, rather than being sold to the black man by an ignorant mother.

Nella mia vita, l'educazione è stata la mia unica salvezza.

In my life, education has been my only salvation.

La parola mafia, derivando dall'arabo "maha", e significando caverna, fa dei mafiosi i cavernicoli, o anche impropriamente detti trogloditi.

Being "maha" the Arab root of the word mafia, and meaning cave, makes mafia people the cavemen, also known as troglodytes.

L'egoismo e l'egocentrismo umano portano a considerare i cani, fedeli amici dell'uomo, come meri oggetti piuttosto che come veri e propri esseri viventi. Infatti, l'uomo tende con troppa facilità a dimenticare che, sebbene addomesticato, il cane conservi ancora un forte istinto animale e di gruppo, reminescenza della vita di branco allo stato brado. Troppo spesso si vedono cani soli che non vengono mai portati al parco per cani, ove poter esser lasciati liberi di formare un branco, anche solo per pochissimo tempo, quindi di poter giocare o passare del tempo anche assieme ai propri simili.

Egoism and egocentrism lead humans to consider dogs, loyal friends of man, as mere objects rather than real living creatures. In fact, humans tend to forget too easily that, although domesticated, dogs retain a strong animal and pack instinct, which is a reminiscence of life in the wild. Too often we see lonely dogs that are never taken to the dog park, where they can be left free to form a pack, even if only for a short time, and be able to play or spend time together with their fellows too.

E se il bombardamento di Venafro non fosse stato un errore? Sulla vicenda vige ancora segreto di stato, ma si sa che gli Alleati avrebbero dovuto bombardare Montecassino, ove si pensava si nascondessero truppe naziste e nostalgici fascisti in gran quantità. Invece, proprio grazie alla Winter Line ci si rese conto che il nemico era arroccato in un paesino che altrimenti sarebbe passato del tutto inosservato. Avessero gli Alleati bombardato e poi attaccato Montecassino, vi avrebbero trovato solo sei o sette soldati, nulla più. A quel punto i nazisti avrebbero potuto colpire gli Alleati prendendoli alle spalle, assaltandoli da San Pietro Infine e sferrando il loro attacco nei pressi di Cassino, ove le truppe Alleate non avrebbero più avuto via d'uscita. Ovviamente l'imboscata nazista non riuscì e fu un gran fiasco a cui memento c'è ancora oggi il Parco della Memoria Storica di San Pietro Infine.

What if the bombardment of Venafro had not been a mistake? The full story is still secret, but we know that the Allies were supposed to bomb Monte Cassino, where the intelligence thought Nazi and nostalgic Fascist troops hid in large numbers. Instead, thanks to the Winter Line, it was realized that the enemy was sheltering in a small town that otherwise would have passed completely unnoticed. Had the Allies bombarded and then attacked Monte Cassino, they would have found only six or seven soldiers, and nothing more. At that point, the Nazis could have hit the Allies, taking them from behind, storming them from San Pietro Infine, and carrying out the attack near Cassino, where Allied troops would have had no way out. Of course, the Nazi ambush failed, and was a complete fiasco. In memory of such event, still today is possible to visit the WWII Memorial Park at San Pietro Infine.

Non c'è posto per la mafia nel futuro dell'Italia.

There ain't no seat for mafia in the future of Italy.

La cultura del posto fisso in Italia è simile a quella dell'uomo che pensa che la donna sia un oggetto di sua proprietà per cui è puttana se lo lascia e l'uomo per cui lo lascia è un pezzo di merda per virtù del parallelismo creatosi dall'egocentrismo italico, per cui tutto è dovuto, secondo un ingoto diritto. Ciò ha fatto si che perfetti incompetenti assumessero ruoli di vitale importanza pubblica e che perfetti idioti si riproducessero come conigli rovinando le vite di intere generazioni.

The culture of a guaranteed job in Italy is similar to that of the man who thinks a woman is an object of his property, and that she is a bitch if she leaves him, as well as the man she leaves him for is a piece of crap. This is due by virtue of a parallelism created by an all Italian egocentrism, whereby everything is due to them, according to an unknown right. This has allowed for perfect incompetents to take vital public roles, and perfect idiots to breed like rabbits, ruining the lives of entire generations.

Tua madre vuole venderti all'uomo nero? Arruolati, troverai conforto tra le mura di mamma Nunziatella, come la chiamano gli ex-allievi!

Your mother wants to sell you to the black man? Joint the Army, you will find solace within the walls of mom Nunziatella, as the alumni call it!

La ricetta per l'Italia è molto semplice, un bel suppostone a tutti i mafiosi e tutto tornerà meglio di com'era prima.

The recipe for Italy it is very simple, a nice big suppository to all mafia gangsters, and everything will better than it was before.

È molto saggio lasciare il bestiame libero di pascolare su e giù per Santa Croce, in particolare ad alta quota, in quanto potrebbero esserci ancora residui bellici nascosti, come mine anti uomo, oltre che alle vipere. In tal senso, i piromani di Venafro hanno fatto un favore alla collettività appiccando fuochi per la montagna, anche se ci sono ancora aree non accessibili neppure agli animali per via della fitta vegetazione spinosa.

It is very wise to let cattle graze freely up and down Mount Holy Cross in Venafro, especially at high altitudes, as there may be still hidden remnants of war, such as land mines, and not only vipers. In this sense, the arsonists of Venafro have done a big favor to the community, by setting fires to the mountain, even if there are still areas inaccessible even to animals, because of the dense thorny vegetation.

Un bel rifugio in legno nei pressi della Torretta Normanna inferiore sarebbe una buona idea ed un gran tocco di classe per il Parco Regionale dell'Olivo di Venafro.

A nice wooden hut by the inferior Norman Tower would be a good idea and a great classy touch for the Olive Regional Park of Venafro.

I prati del Parco Regionale dell'Olivo di Venafro, proprio dietro la cattedrale, sarebbero meglio di Hyde Park a Londra per i bagni di sole, se non fosse per l'immondizia lasciata in giro ovunque dai venafrani.

The meadows of the Olive Regional Park of Venafro, just behind the Cathedral, would be better than Hyde Park in London for sunbathing, if it weren't for the rubbish left lying around everywhere by Venafro's people.

Datasi la sporcizia ed ogetti vari lasciati a segnaletica per il Parco Regionale dell'Olivo di Venafro vien spontaneo domandarsi se esso venga usato come spaccio più che area culturale e ricreativa.

Given the rubbish and other various objects left around Venafro's Olive Regional Park as some kind of markers, makes me wonder whether it is used as a trafficking rather than cultural and recreational area.

Venafro, 222mt, 12000 abitanti, ma dai clacson e dalle cornacchie si direbbe vi sia un morto ogni minuto.

Venafro, 222mt, 12000 inhabitants, but judging by the honking and crows, one would say there is a death every minute.

I droni esistono, sono semplici da usare e costano meno di un parco auto quindi debbono essere dati alle Forze dell'Ordine per migliorane l'efficacia e produttività.

Drones are a reality, simple to use and cost less than a car park, therefore must be given to law enforcement to improve efficiency and productivity.

Personalmente, in virtù della reale situazione a Venafro, equiparerei gli abusi dei clacson alla guida in stato di ebrezza con relativo ritiro di patente e pagamento delle somme dovute per riaverla. La patente di guida è infatti un privilegio, non un diritto e le scimmie infatti se ne stanno sugli alberi, non al volante.

Personally, due to the real situation in Venafro, I would compare honking abuses to driving thrill, with the consequent withdrawal of the driving license, and the payment a fair amount to get it back. In fact, the driver's license is a privilege, not a right, as much as monkeys stay up on trees, not behind the wheel.

I dati sul femminicidio in Italia parlano chiaro: è la vergogna italiana al cospetto del mondo, retaggio di una cultura arabo-mafiosa, da cui deriva la radice stessa del termine mafia, ossia dall'arabo "maha".

Data on femicide in Italy are clear: it is the shame of Italy before the world, a legacy of an Arab-mafia culture, where the very root of the word mafia comes from, i.e. the Arabic word "maha."

I mafiosi si oppongono all'educazione in quanto una donna in grado di leggere e capire l'inglese potrebbe aprire gli occhi sulla reale sua condizione e come essa venga considerata dalle Nazioni Unitie.

Mafia members are opposed to education because, once a woman can read and understand English, she could realize her real condition, and how that is regarded by the United Nations.

E come sempre, signori e signore, come da migliaia di anni a questa parte, sarà proprio in Italia, nel mezzo del Mediterraneo (Media Terra) che si giocherà la partita tra l'Europa civilizzata e il resto del mondo selvaggio. Più si scende, più fa caldo.

And as usual, ladies and gentlemen, as for thousands of years, it will be right here in Italy, in the middle of the Mediterranean (Land in the middle) that the game between civilized Europe and the rest of the uncivilized world will be played. The farther south one goes, the hotter it gets.

Se la spada "Gladio" è il simbolo dell'antica Roma come istituzione, il pino è senza dubbio il simbolo della terra di Roma.

If the sword "Gladius" is the symbol of ancient Rome as an institution, the pine is undoubtedly symbol of the land of Rome.

Il notariato va assolutamente liberalizzato.

The Italian notary system must be absolutely liberalized.

Il concetto di casa popolare va assolutamente debellato. Gli organi predisposti all'assistenza sociale possono lavorare con privati per trovare le soluzioni migliori, anche mediante forme di sgravi fiscali. Lo Stato non deve assolutamente essere coinvolto direttametne nelle edificazioni né tantomeno nella gestione di tali alloggi.

The concept of public housing has got to be completely eradicated. The organs designed to social assistance can work with the private sector to find the best solutions, including forms of tax relief. The Government should not be involved directly in building such accommodations or in its management.

Dalla mia esperienza di vissuto personale negli Stati Uniti, posso testimoniare che l'assicurazione medica, inclusa quella odontoiatrica, costava meno oltreoceano che la ritenuta sanitaria in busta paga di un impiegato in Italia.

From my personal experience in the United States, I can testify that medical insurance, including dentistry, cost less overseas than the public health plan withholdings on the paycheck of Italian employees in Italy.

Per i libertari la ricetta è semplice: - stato = - tasse = + libertà = - ladri = solo controlli e reale implementazaione della Legge, ossia niente mafia = niente pistole ma solo manganelli per tenere l'ordine pubblico, come per i Bobby inglesi.

For libertarians, the recipe is simple: - state = - taxes = + freedom = - thieves = only controls and real implementation of the law, i.e. no mafia = no guns, but only batons to keep public order, like the British bobbies.

Berlusconi non hai tutti i torti nel sostenere che i tempi della Giustizia italiani non sono più appropriati ai tempi e alle esigenze contemporanee.

Berlusconi has a point arguing that the timing of Italian Justice is no longer appropriate to modern times and contemporary needs.

Il mondo è pieno di paradossi. Venafro è una città i cui abitanti si ostinano a voler vivere come in un villaggio nel Corno d'Africa, sebbene gli africani facciano di tutto per venire a vivere in città.

The world is full of paradoxes. Venafro is a city whose inhabitants do anything to keep living like in a village in the Horn of Africa, although Africans do anything possible to come live in the city.

Sognare è l'unico vero scopo dell'esistere.

Dreaming is the only real purpose of existence.

La mafia fa del naturale timore di morire la propria leva. E a me onestamente vien solo da ridere per quanto sono scimmie i mafiosi e gli omertosi che ne appoggiano l'operato.

Mafia makes of the natural fear of dying its lever. And honestly, I can only laugh for mafia members are just like monkeys, as well as the silent accomplices who facilitate its work.

Temo anche le cornacchie siano indispettite verso l'uomo solo perché hanno fame, tanto quanto i lupi che sono costretti a cercare prede sempre più a valle, avvicinandosi troppo all'uomo. L'uomo infatti è talmente egoista da non comprendere che in Terra non esiste solo lui e che sebbene gli faccia comodo occupare quanto più spazio possibile impadronendosene, ciò non servirà a terner lontano l'ira di Madre Natura una volta che questa sia stata abusata oltre il limite di sopportazione.

I'm afraid even the crows have grown irritated because of man, just because they're hungry, as much as the wolves, which are forced to seek preys at increasingly, lower altitudes, getting too close to man. Man is so selfish to not understand that he is not alone on Earth, and that despite it feels always more comfortable to occupy as much space as possible for his needs, this will not help keeping away the wrath of mother nature once it has been abused beyond the limit of endurance.

Sarebbe il caso che qualche uomo o donna di buona volontà liberasse delle quaglie su Monte Santa Croce per cominciare a ricreare un accenno di ecosistema. Ne avessi le risorse, lo farei io stesso. Se poi qualcuno volesse comprare delle quaglie, ma fosse incapacitato ad andare in montagna a liberarle, sarei più che felice di portarcele io di persona.

It would be the case that a man or woman of goodwill released some quails on Mount Holy Cross in Venafro in order to recreate a hint of ecosystem. If I had the resources I would do it myself. Then, if someone wanted to buy some quails, but was incapacitated to go up the mountain to free them, I'd be more than happy to do it for them.

Quasi sicuramente, anche l'origine della tradizione del "presepio" è da attribuirsi a Ponzio Pilato, che deve essersi ispirato alla Venafro antica come scenografia del presepio stesso. Ciò potrebbe averne causato la distruzione e la ricostruzione con sembianze del tutto identiche alle rappresentazioni del presepio, con il monte, il grotto e i pastori.

Almost certainly, the origin of the tradition of the "Nativity" or "Presepio" is also to be attributed to Pontius Pilate, who must have been inspired by the ancient Venafro for the scenic design. This may have caused the destruction and reconstruction of Venafro, looking identical to the representation of the Nativity scene, with the mount, the grotto and the shepherds.

Mi verrebbe spontaneo dire che mi vergogno di essere nato. Eppure, nonostante tutto, non riesco a credere quanto sia bella Venafro.

I would naturally say that I was ashamed to be born. Yet, in spite of everything, I can't believe how beautiful Venafro is.

Faccio finta di non sapere perché in Italia si piangono i morti anzicché i vivi.

I pretend not knowing why in Italy people mourn the dead instead of the living ones.

Un paio di giorni in cella farebbero bene a chiunque, datosi che il carcere è da considerarsi innanzitutto una struttura educativa e correttiva prim'ancora che penitenziaria. Quando il carcere non funziona in tal senso, può purtroppo degenerare in sovraffollamento, ma solo perché la società al di fuori del carcere stesso fallisce nell'educare non solo la propria popolazione carceraria, ma l'intera collettività.

A couple of days in jail would do well to anyone, as prisons are to be considered first and foremost educational and corrective institutions, not only jails. When prisons do not work in this respect, they can unfortunately degenerate into overcrowding, but only because the society outside fails to educate not only its prison population, but the entire community as well.

Il grado di salute di un qualsiasi nucleo cittadino lo si misura non tanto dalla qualità del manto stradale, dalla pulizia del suolo urbano o dall'efficienza dei trasporti, quanto dalla sua struttura ospedaliera.

The overall level of wellness of a community is measured not so much by the quality of road surface, the cleaning of urban environments or transport efficiency, but by its hospital.

Una Costituzione Europea senza alcun riferimento religioso potrebbe essere la soluzione giusta, purché l'Europa si faccia carico di rinegoziare i Patti Lateranensi al suo interno. Una volta approvata a Brussel, eventuali conflitti con le Costituzioni degli Stati Membri potranno essere emendate direttamente a livello Nazionale dagli Organi competenti.

A European Constitution, without any religious reference, might be the right solution, provided that Europe will assume to renegotiate the Lateran pacts within. Once approved in Brussel, any conflicts with Member States' constitutions may be amended directly at national level, by the competent bodies.

Ormai siamo giunti al bivio da troppo tempo, come ai tempi di Mosè, o andiamo avanti o si torna indietro, accettandone tutte le conseguenze.

We paused at a crossroads for too long, as in the days of Moses, now either we continue forward or go back, accepting all consequences.

Per l'ennesima volta, si ribadisce come mediante privatizzazioni, lo Stato italiano potrebbe estinguere il debito interno con una semplicissima operazione di Swapping, anche nei confronti delle PMI e senza ulteriore indebitamento da aste di titoli pubblici. Ma gli italiani ci arriveranno mai a capire la finanza? Si tratterebbe insomma di pagare gli italiani con azioni di società privatizzate come le Poste e le Ferrovie dello Stato. Poi essi potranno essere liberi di farci quello che vogliono.

For the umpteenth time, I reiterate how, through privatization, the Italian Government could extinguish its domestic debt, with a simple swap operation, even for small and medium size businesses, and without the need for further borrowing through bond auctions. But will Italians ever understand finance? Basically, all it would take was paying back Italians with shares of the newly privatized companies, such as the Italian Post and the National Railways. Then citizens will be free to do what they want of it.

Sono anni ormai che ripeto sempre le stesse cose e mi sono proprio stufato dell'ignoranza tutt'intorno a me. Per questo la guerra è sempre un'eventualità da non sottovalutare mai.

For years now I have been repeating the same things over an over again. Finally, I'm just too tired of the ignorance all around me. For this reason wars are always a possibility that cannot be underestimated.

Piangere dopo non serve a niente, come non serve a niente piangere i morti.

Crying afterwards is worthless, just like crying for the dead.

Meglio essere orfanelli che venire da una famiglia morbosa.

Better to be orphans than living in a morbid family.

I cittadini privilegiati, come ad esempio i membri delle Forze dell'Ordine, delle Forze Armate ed i licenziatari statali, ossia coloro che godono di una particolare licenza come nel caso degli alcolici, dei tabacchi e delle armi da fuoco, debbono essere soggetti a pene più severe in caso di mancato rispetto della Legge, anche e soprattutto quando non sono in servizio, previa la sospensione delle loro licenze o dei loro incarichi di servizio pubblico.

Privileged citizens, such as members of the Police, the Armed Forces, and the Government, like those holding a special license, as in the case of alcohol, tobacco and firearms, should be subject to stricter penalties in case of non-compliance with the Law, especially when they are not in service, including the suspension of their licenses and public service roles.

Se politicamente parlando l'Europa è il futuro, dal punto di vista di alte possibilità speculative e sviluppo economico il futuro è l'Africa. E l'Italia da questo punto di vista è avvantaggiata dalla sua posizione geografica.

If it's true that, politically speaking, Europe is the future; from the point of view of high speculative opportunities and economic development, the future is Africa. And, in this prospective, Italy greatly benefits by its natural geographical position.

A volte non comprendo proprio i giudici. Infatti, se è vero che il falso in bilancio in Italia non è più reato, rimane pur sempre l'imputabilità di corruzione, concussione ed omissione di atti d'ufficio. Dopotutto il falso in bilancio non è il crimine ma la prova stessa del crimine, ossia della corruzione.

Sometimes I do not understand judges. In fact, while it is true that ccounting frauds are no longer a crime in Italy, yet they are still crimes of corruption and bribery or other abuses. After all, accounting frauds are not a crime itself, but the evidence itself, namely corruption.

Come si fa a spiegare agli ignoranti che le persone che parlano più lingue, quattro ad esempio (italiano, inglese, spagnolo e napoletano) hanno un udito molto fine, sviluppato nel corso di anni di pratica nel riconoscere suoni diversi e pertanto sono molto più sensibili dei monolingua ai suoni ed ai rumori ambientali? Venafro per esempio, con Santa Croce che funge da cassa risonante, è un inferno per via dei clacson automobilistici e ferroviari, senza parlare delle campane che sfonderebbero i timpani pure a King Kong e senza parlare dei gravi danni che vengono inflitti agli infanti che purtroppo debbono vivere in una città in cui a nessuno sembri importare dell'inquinamento né atmosferico né sonoro e figuriamoci ambientale.

How do you explain to ignorant people that those who speak multiple languages, four for example (Italian, English, Spanish and Neapolitan) have a very fine hearing, developed over years of practice in recognizing different sounds; therefore the are much more sensitive than monolingual to sounds and ambient noise? Venafro for example, where Mount Holy Cross acts as a resonant box is hell, because of the honking cars and trains, not to mention the bells that would break down even King Kong's eardrums. Let's not even mention the serious damage being inflicted to infants, who unfortunately have to live in a city where nobody seems to care about air or sound pollution, nor even environmental.

Al 2013 in Italia vige ancora il nepotismo.

As of 2013, in Italy there is still nepotism.

La guerra altro non è che la naturale ed inevitabile conseguenza del malfunzionamento della Legge e della Giustizia in genere.

War is nothing more than the natural and inevitable consequence of failure complying with the Law and Justice in general.

In ultima analisi, i mafiosi perseverano pensando che tanto non potranno mica arrestarli tutti.

Ultimately, mafia members and gangsters believe they can persist as they cannot be all arrested.

Forse i mafiosi non hanno tutti i torti nel sostenere che non potranno essere tutti arrestati o si dovrebbero svuotare città intere. Sicuramente però li si potrà tutti chippare, trattandoli da bestie quali realmente sono.

Maybe mafia members are right arguing they cannot all be arrested or whole cities should be emptied. But surely they can all be chipped, and treated as the beasts they really are.

Personalmente, credo di aver saldato il conto col Governo italiano divulgando gratis i miei scritti ed i miei studi per anni. All'Italia infatti dovevo parte della mia formazione, frutto dei miei anni presso la Scuola Militare Nunziatella di Napoli. Anche l'educazione infatti ha un costo e alla Patria ho tornato solo ciò che era dovuto.

Personally, I think I've paid my bill with the Italian Government, by spreading my writings and my studies for years and for free. In fact, I owed Italy part of my training, result of the years spent at the Nunziatella Military School in Naples. However, also education has a cost, and I returned my country of origin only what was owed.

Tutti i parchi nazionali e regionali italiani dovrebbero essere collegati mediante corridoi naturali al fine di garantire continuità di spostamento agli animali che vi ci abitano.

All Italian national and regional parks should be connected by natural corridors to ensure continuity of movement for the animals that inhabit them.

Chi alleva il bestiame non può assolutamente macellarlo.

People who raise livestock cannot slaughter them.

Col tempo e l'esperienza ho capito che molte catastrofi naturali non sono affatto dovute ad armi o tecnologie militari ignote, bensì solo all'ignoranza ed all'incuria dell'uomo. Nel mondo animale, non si conosce il concetto di autodistruzione, nel senso che prede e predatori benché si caccino stanno molto attenti allo stato di salute generale di entrambi. Solo l'uomo invece pensa di essere al di sopra delle leggi della natura, ignorandole con l'arroganza di abusarne a suo piacimento, cercando altrove il colpevole delle proprie malefatte.

With time and experience, I realized that many natural disasters are not caused by weapons or unknown military technology, but only by ignorance and carelessness of man. In the animal world, there is no concept of self-destruction, in the sense that preys and predators, although they hunt and look after each other, are very attentive to the overall health of both. Instead, only man thinks he is above the laws of nature, with the most extraordinary arrogance of abusing it to his liking, and even looking elsewhere for the culprit of their wrongdoings.

Il vero insegnamento della legge dell'attrazione forse è quello di far realizzare la più banale, eppur più saggia, delle combinazioni delle coppie umane. Infatti, combinare contemporaneamente diversità e similitudini in terra non è da poco. A mio parere, uomini bruni con occhi marroni starebbero meglio con donne bionde ed occhi azzurri e viceversa. Donne con capelli bruno chiari ed occhi chiare andrebbero bene con uomini mori ed occhi marroni e viceversa. Per le altre possibili conbinazioni al momento non ho ancora una soluzione definitiva.

Maybe the true teaching of the law of attraction is to realize the more banal, yet most wise, of human pair combinations. In fact, combining both diversity and similarities on Earth is not an easy task. In my opinion, brown-haired men with brown eyes would be better with blond and blue-eyed women, and vice versa. Women with brown hair and light colored eyes should go well with black-haired, brown eyes men, and vice versa. For all other possible combinations, at the moment I still don't have a definitive solution.

Temo le campagne disinformative riguardo l'AIDS possano essere state volutamente propagandate per celare la malattia stessa, per paura di esserne stati contagiati. La cosa potrebbe essere molto preoccupante qualora, indipendentemente dai propri studi o meno, si abbiano avuti comportamenti sessuali già ritenuti pericolosi per via della diffusione delle malattie sessualmente trasmittibili (MST).

I'm afraid the uninformative campaigns about AIDS may have been intentionally being touted to conceal the disease itself, for fear of having been infected. It could be very worrying if, independently on one's studies or not, a large part of the population had a sexual behavior already considered dangerous for the spreading of sexually transmitted disease (STD.)

I clacson di Venafro sembrano di clienti alla ricerca di una puttana, quasi a dire: "Riec'eur ah bott'".. ma all'AIDS po' chi c'penz? Senza menzionare che la forte presenza di militari e caserme, sebbene in servizio d'ordine, e che nonostante il numero non riescano a garantire il più banale del rispetto della legalità, è noto statisticamente aumentare certi rischi. Venafro poi è nota essere la porta d'accesso al Molise, per cui è pesantemente trafficata da camionisti, altra categoria a rischio e con l'aggravarsi della condizione economica, la città diventa sempre più vulnerabile al diffondersi di malattie veneree.

The honking in Venafro seems like customers looking for a whore, as if to say, "Ten bucks a fuck." But what about AIDS? That's without mentioning that the strong presence of military personnel and barracks, although as military police, which despite their numbers fail to ensure the most trivial respect for legality, is known to increase certain risks statistically. Venafro is also known to be the gateway to Molise, therefore heavily trafficked by truckers, another at-risk category, and with the worsening economic conditions, the city is becoming increasingly vulnerable to the spread of venereal diseases.

L'uomo è responsabile di aver rotto gli equilibri naturali e della biosfera, quindi all'uomo spetta il compito di ristabilirli.

Man is responsible for breaking the natural balance of the biosphere, therefore is man's duty to restore it.

Come si dice in napoletano, ormai siamo al tempo in cui: "Ah mignott fa' riec'eur a'bot. Oh gigolò, bast ko rai a'magnà."

As they say in Naples, we are now at the time when, "whores charge ten bucks a fuck, and gigolos only ask for a meal."

Io cambierei la ninna nanna da uomo nero a cavaliere.

I'd change the Italian bed time song "ninna nanna" from "black man" to "knight."

Certo però che anche fare la puttana o il puttano ha un costo. 36 euro di ticket ogni due settimane per le analisi sono 72 euro, ossia 7 botte a 10 euro e qualche mancia. Poi ci sono le spese per l'affitto, la corrente, il gas, la lingerie, ma i profilattici almeno si possono mettere a carico del cliente, cui si può anche far pagare qualche olio lubrifante a seguito del mestiere usurante. Si stima che per coprire tali spese ci vogliano almeno 60 botte al mese solo per garantirsi l'esistenza, ed ovviamente i consorzi sono sconsigliati in quanto darebero troppo all'occhio e non possibili per legge. Poi bisognerà stare attenti a non sforare la soglia massima fissata dal fisco per la non dichiarazione dei redditi, che con 60 botte al mese procurerà un incasso di 7200 euro l'anno, senza includere le 7 botte al mese solo per le spese mediche, ma quelle sono scaricabili. Certo, i soldi facendo il mestiere non si potranno certo fare, ma quantomeno servirà a campare in attesa di migliore impiego. Con l'età poi il mestiere non servirà neppure più per la sussistenza, ma chi lo fa il problema non se lo pone in quanto ha altro a cui pensare, come ad esempio cosa mettere in tavola tra una botta e l'altra.

Funny enough, also being a male or female whore has a cost. 36 euros in medical tickets every two weeks for checkups is 72 euros, i.e. 7 fucks at 10 euros each and little tips. Then there is rent, electricity, gas, lingerie, but at least condoms can be charged to the customers, who can also pay for some Vaseline, due to the arduous job. It is estimated that to cover such expenditures it takes at least 60 fucks a month, just to secure one's existence, and of course, consortia are not recommended because too impudent, and not allowed by law. Then one must also be careful not to break the maximum threshold set by the Italian IRS, for not filing tax returns, which with 60 fucks a month generates proceeds of 7200 euros a year, not including the 7 fucks a month needed only for medical expenses, but those are deductible. Sure, one will never become reach by doing the oldest job on Earth, but at least it will serve to make ends meet, while waiting for a better employment. With age though prostitution will not even assure subsistence, but who cares. After all, who does it does not worry about it, as he or she has other things to worry about, such as what to put on the table between a fuck and the other.

Tecnicamente, per via del suo secondo matrimonio con Aicha, di sei anni, Maometto ai giorni nostri sarebbe considerato pedofilo.

Technically speaking, because of his second marriage to Aisha, of age six, Muhammad would be considered a pedophile nowaday.

La spada "Gladio" ricorda nella forma i gladioli, la stessa che mozzò il capo a San Nicandro a Venafro e Cicerone a Formia e sempre per questo motivo, i gladioli sono i fiori dei morti, in quanto la spada "Gladio" è sporca di molto sangue.

The sword "Gladius" resembles the shape of the gladiolus flower, the same that cut off the heads of St. Nicander in Venafro and Cicero in Formia, and for this reason, gladioli are the flowers of the dead, as the sword "Gladius" is very bloody.

A Venafro, i due blocchi di Villa Pilato, con intorno il liceo classico, la chiesa del Carmine e la cattedrale rappresentano il quartiere ebraico-cristiano della città. Ciò per via del mosaico di Villa Pilato con la stella di David e gli affreschi della cattedrale con scritte in ebraico.

In Venafro, the two blocks of Pilate's Villa, surrounded by the classical lyceum, the Carmel church and the cathedral, represent the Jewish-Christian district of the city. This because of the mosaic of Villa Pilate with the Star of David, and the frescoes of the Cathedral with Hebrew inscriptions.

Invecchiare è come tornare all'innocenza, ossia ricordare com'era quando si era bambini.

Aging is like returning to innocence, meaning remembering how it was when one was a child.

Per puro caso, all'ospedale di Isernia si è notata una pianta identica alla stella alpina piantata a Venafro. Si è pertanto supposto che quella di Isernia dovesse essere una varietà autoctona e più antica di stella alpina. Le due varietà sono identiche nella infiorescenza, sebbene presentino una leggera varizione genetica nella forma delle foglie. Quella piantata a Venafro infatti ha delle foglie più sottili ed allungate rispetto quella ritrovata ad Isernia, con foglie più piccole ed allargate. Inoltre, un fatto molto particolare è che la varietà rinvenuta ad Isernia, cresceva nei pressi delle rovine romane presenti all'ospedale e che, sempre ad Isernia, nella villa comunale, vi è collocata una mezza colonna romana, su un piedistallo su cui è raffigurata proprio la stella alpina.

By pure chance, at the Isernia Civil Hospital, I noticed a grass identical to the edelweiss I planted in Venafro. It was therefore assumed that the one found in Isernia could be a native and oldest variety of edelweiss. The two varieties have identical inflorescence, although presenting a slight genetical variation in the form of their leaves. The type planted in Venafro has thinner and more elongated leaves than the one found in Isernia, presenting smaller and more enlarged leaves. Also, a very interesting fact is that the variety found in Isernia, grew close to the ancient ruins by the hospital and that, always in Isernia, in the town park, there is a half-Roman column, placed on a pedestal on which is engraved and noticeable just the six leaved edelweiss .

E se il napoletano derivasse dall'osco più che dal latino?

What if the Neapolitan language derived more from Oscan than Latin?

Credo che le lingue indo-europee si siano formate per distaccarsi ed allontanarsi dalle lingue semitiche come per sfuggire dall'origine della mafia, che deriva linguisticamente dall'arabo.

I believe that the Indo-European languages have evolved to detach and move away from the Semitic language, as to escape from the origin of the mafia, which linguistically derives from Arabic.

La storia del sud Europa è simile al far-West americano. La colonizzazione degli Stati Uniti cominciò infatti dall'Est, fu quindi duro imporre la Legge man mano che i pionieri avanzavano verso l'Ovest. Agli sceriffi e vici-sceriffi, senza l'esercito, risultava difficile tenere sotto controllo la situazione, eppure essi sapevano che col tempo sarebbero arrivati i rinforzi, ed oggi l'Ovest americano sembra aver dimenticato del tutto quei giorni, sfidando l'Est in termini di sviluppo e progresso. La stessa sorte toccherà al Meridione europeo, che attualmente sembrerebbe in balia del caos e dell'illegalità, sebbene ciò sia solo un fatto temporaneo e destinato a mutare molto presto, nonostante l'esistenza di mafiosi o terroristi locali che vantano d'essere briganti e banditi da quattro soldi.

The history of southern Europe is similar to the far-West. In fact, the colonization of the United States began from the East, and it was hard at first to enforce the law, as the pioneers were advancing west. For sheriffs and vice-sheriffs, without the army, it was difficult to keep the situation under control, yet they knew over time reinforcements would arrive. Today, the American West seems to have forgotten those days, rivaling the East in terms of development and progress. The same sorts await southern Europe, which currently seems to be at the mercy of chaos and lawlessness. Although, this is only temporary, and intended to change very soon, despite the presence of mafia – terrorists – who praise being shoestring robbers and bandits.

C'è un filo sottilissimo che lega l'Italia all'America ed in particolar modo a New York e che non passa necessariamente per Colombo né Vespucci. Infatti, non solo Giulio Cesare fu colui che iniziò il domino Romano sulla Britannia, ma è anche uno dei padri della lingua inglese, per via dell'invenzione del famoso Cifrario di Cesare, ossia del metodo di criptare l'alfabeto, da cui deriva il duplice alfabeto scritto e fonetico dell'inglese utilizzato ancora oggi. Come se tutto ciò non bastasse, una delle province romane in Britannia sottratte al controllo dei celti era proprio York, da cui prende il nome New York.

There is a thin thread binding Italy and America, especially in New York, and that does not necessarily pass through Columbus or Vespucci. In fact, not only Julius Caesar was the one who started the Roman domination of Britannia, but he is also one of the fathers of the English language. This is due to the invention of the famous Caesar cipher, i.e. the method of encrypting the alphabet, hence the dual written and phonetic alphabet of English, still used today. And as if all that wasn't enough, one of the very first Roman provinces in Britain reclaimed from the control of the Celts was York, whereas the name New York.

Venafro è intrinsicamente legata alla Gran Bretagna non solo per via della Torricella Normanna, bensì anche per via degli alabastri di Nottingham conservati presso il Castello Pandone e raffiguranti la passione di Cristo. Cosa molto interessante è che se si analizza il "Gioiello di Alfredo," commissionato appunto dal re Alfredo il Grande, cresimato a Roma da Papa Leone IV e nato nell'Oxforshire, si può notare la somiglianza di quello stile reffigurativo poi riscontrato negli alabastri. Alfredo il Grande fu infatti responsabile di ordinare la traduzione di diversi manoscritti dal latino in inglese al fine di risolvere una certa carenza culturale che si stava diffondendo in Inghilterra per via della decadenza della diffusione della lingua latina. È interessante come, ancora oggi, proprio Oxford sia considerata una dei principali centri d'istruzione a livello mondiale. Inoltre, fu proprio Alfredo il Grande a rendere obbligatoria l'istruzione in Inghilterra ed a facilitare la diffusione di diversi testi sacri trascritti in inglese per una più facile lettura e divulgazione. Come se non bastasse, un suo successore, re Edoardo il Confessore, fece cominciare i lavori di costruzione dell'Abbazia di Westminster, in stile romanico, che è proprio lo stile della Cattedrale o Duomo di Venafro.

Venafro is intrinsically tied to Britain not only because of the Norman Tower, but also because of the Nottingham alabasters held at the Pandone Castle, and depicting the passion of Christ. A very interesting thing is that, if one looks at the "Alfred's jewel," commissioned by King Alfred the Great - confirmed in Rome by Pope Leo IV and born in Oxforshire – it is possible to notice a style similarity with the representations of the alabaster figures. Alfred the Great was also responsible for ordering the translation of several manuscripts from the Latin into English, in order to solve a certain cultural gap that was spreading in England, due to the decadence of the Latin language. It is interesting how, even today, Oxford is a major cultural center worldwide. In addition, it was Alfred the Great to make education compulsory in England, and to promote the spreading of various sacred texts transcribed in English for easier reading and distribution. As if that weren't enough, one of his successors, King Edward the Confessor, began the construction of the Westminster Abbey, in Romanesque style, which is precisely the style of the Cathedral or Dome of Venafro.

Col senno del poi, ed in virtù degli avvenimenti vissuti ai giorni odierni, si potrebbe dire che "La fattoria degli animali" di Geroge Orwell fosse una parodia della cultura mafioso-terroristica, come a voler anticipare le sorti del capovolgimento dell'ordine naturale delle posizioni sociali in cui si trova a vivere l'uomo. Alla fine infatti, come animali, i mafiosi ed i terroristi finiranno per uccidersi l'un l'altro, in quanto essi pensano ed agiscono contro natura. Tra l'altro, tutto ciò era già stato anche anticipato dal crollo del comunismo.

With the hindsight of then, and by virtue of the events lived these current days, one could say that "Animal farm" by George Orwell was a parody of the mafia-like and terrorist culture. He tried to anticipate the sorts of the reversal of the social, natural order in which we all live. At the end, like animals, mafia members, gangsters and terrorists will end up killing each other, as they think and act against nature. Among other things, this had already been anticipated by the collapse of communism.

In letteratura Cesare è certamente ricordato per aver scritto il "De bello Gallico" a seguito delle sue vittorie in Gallia. Storicamente però egli è meglio ricordato tra le persone comuni per le sue avventure in Egitto con Cleopatra. In virtù della sua fine, assassinato a Roma, con le seguenti vicissitudini del povero Ponzio Pilato con Gesù Cristo, ed il crollo dell'impero romano, bisogna ammettere che forse aveva le idee un po' confuse. Infatti, dall'Africa e dal Medio Oriente importò a Roma i semi di quella cultura all'epoca definita "saracena", poi evolutasi in arabica e degenerata con le varie invasioni arabe del sud Europa, con residui ancora oggi visibili sottoforma di cultura mafiosa. Ai Galli invece, per mezzo dell'invenzione del cifrario, cui molto probabilmente è dovuto il suo successo, regalò il segreto del criptaggio che, una volta compreso, divenne parte integrante della lingua dei celti. Duemila anni dopo, il mondo si trova ancora una volta ad essere conteso tra civiltà e barbarie.

In literature, Caesar is certainly remembered for having written the "De bello Gallico" following his victories in Gaul. Historically, however, he is better remembered among ordinary people for his adventures in Egypt with Cleopatra. By virtue of his end, murdered in Rome, the vicissitudes of poor Pontius Pilate with Jesus Christ, and the collapse of the Roman Empire, one has to admit that maybe he had somewhat confused ideas. In fact, from Africa and the Middle East, he imported to Rome the seeds of that culture at the time defined "Saracen," which later evolved into Arabic, and then degenerated with the various Arab invasions of southern Europe, with remnants still visible today, in the form of mafia-like culture. On the other hand, by mean of the invention of the cipher, which is most likely the key to his success, he gave the Gaul the secret of encryption that, once understood, became part of the language of the Celts. Two thousand years later, the world is once again contented between civilization and barbarism.

Col senno del poi, ed in virtù degli avvenimenti vissuti ai giorni odierni, si potrebbe dire che "1984" di Geroge Orwell preannunciasse i timori dell'autore che percepì i cambiamenti che avrebbero persuaso il mondo a fronte delle sue future sfide. Sotto molti aspetti, Orwell centrò in pieno sia l'evolversi dei governi, sia degli scenari geopolitici futuri. Dai suoi scritti però si evince la sua paura più intima di fronte a tali sfide e scenari. Orwell non riuscì a comprendere però che il concetto di grande fratello altro non fosse che l'evoluzione proprio del naturale istinto protettivo di un fratello maggiore nei confronti del minore, al passo con le tecnologie moderne. Orwell infatti non considerò che la stessa tecnologia che tanto gli incuteva timore sarebbe stata alla portata anche di mafiosi e terroristi, per cui sarebbe divenuto inevitabile, come sempre nel corso della storia, che i giusti e i saggi l'avrebbero usata e contesa con i cattivi proprio per proteggere la propria prole in un mondo in continuo cambiamento. Per giunta, come diceva Darwin, è colui che meglio si adatta ad avere maggiori possibilità di sopravvivere.

With the hindsight of then, and by virtue of the events lived these current days, one could say that "1984" by George Orwell forecasted the author's fears, who perceived the changes that would have persuaded the world to meet its future challenges. In many ways, Orwell hit fully both the evolution of Governments, and future geopolitical scenarios. His writings, in fact, show his innermost fears facing those challenges and scenarios. Orwell failed to understand, however, that the concept of big brother was nothing but the evolution of the natural protective instinct of an elder brother to the younger, in harmony with the latest technology. Orwell did not consider that the same, much feared technology would have been within reach of mobsters and terrorists as well. For such reason, it would have become inevitable, as always throughout history, that the righteous and wise men had used and feud it with the bad guys, just to protect their offspring in a changing world. Furthermore, as Darwin said, it is the one that is best suited to have a better chance to survive.

Sopravvivere alla grande crisi economica del XXI secolo è un'impresa colossale in virtù delle innumerevoli variabili da comprendere e calcolare, stando ben attenti a non cadere negli stessi vecchi errori precedentemente commessi e che portarono alle due guerre del XX secolo.

Surviving the great economic crisis of the 21st century is a colossal undertaking, by virtue of the countless variables to understand and calculate, being cautious not to fall into the same old mistakes previously committed, and that led to the two World Wars of the 20th century.

Dopo aver fatto testmento, mi sono reso conto che nella vita, ad un certo momento, è necessario trarre le proprie conclusioni. Nel mio caso, ad esempio, ho scelto che una volta esaurite tutte le scorte energetiche per la diplomazia, la solidarietà, la pazienza e la comprensione, è lecito e necessario usare le bombe per risolvere le questioni socio-economiche che altrimenti finerebbero per affliggere pure coloro che per l'appunto sono più sensibili e responsabili verso il prossimo di quanto si possa credere.

After doing my testament, I realized that, at some point in life, one needs to draw their own conclusions. In my case, for example, I chose that once all the energy reserves for diplomacy, solidarity, patience and understanding have been depleted, it may be necessary to use bombs to solve the socio-economical issues that would otherwise afflict precisely those who are more sensitive and responsible towards others than one might believe.

Se la verità è un'offesa, allora a me piace offendere.

If truth is an offense, then I like offending.

La lotta agli integralisti islamici e a tutti coloro che ne appoggiano ideologie e fini ultimi riguarda molto profondamente l'Italia, ma non per via della sua partecipazione alla coalizione interforze schierata nella lotta ed al contrasto di tali attività. Infatti, come più volte ribadito, il termine "mafia", tanto noto e caro agli italiani, deriva linguisticamente proprio dall'arabo "maha", ossia caverna o grotta oscura. Il fatto che i mafiosi siano quindi dei cavernicoli non è in sé un fattore di rischio, bensì l'aggravante delle loro azioni illecite. Infatti, a cominciare dall'evasione fiscale, il mercato nero è proprio ciò che fornisce ai terroristi le risorse finanziarie per poter vivere e tramare al buio, nelle grotte per l'appunto, come Osama bin Laden. Gli italiani dunque, che si rendono colpevoli di evasione fiscale, finanziano direttamente il terrorismo internazionale e come risaputo, la Legge non ammette ignoranza.

The fight against Islamic fundamentalists, and all those supporting their ideologies and ultimate purpose, relates to Italy very deeply. Not only because of Italy's participation in the international joint coalition deployed in the fight, and to the contrast of such activities. In fact, as repeatedly stated, the term "mafia," well known and dear to Italians, derives from the Arabic term "maha," meaning cave or dark grotto. The fact that mobsters are therefore cavemen is not by itself a risk factor, but the aggravation of their illegal actions. In fact, starting with tax evasion, the black market is precisely what provides financial resources to terrorists, to live and plot in the dark, just like Osama bin Laden. Italians, who make themselves guilty of tax evasion, directly finance international terrorism and, as well known, the Law does not allow for ignorance.

Forse che il Presidente George W. Bush, con la sua famosa affermazione "missione compiuta" si riferisse proprio al quadro del pittore italiano Paolo Uccello intitolato "San Giorgio e il drago"? Dopotutto, Uccello dipense il drago proprio fuori la sua grotta oscura, ossia "maha" in arabo e "mafia" in italiano.

Maybe President George W. Bush, with his famous statement, "mission accomplished," was referring to the painting of the Italian painter Paolo Uccello titled, "St. George and the dragon." After all, Uccello painted the dragon just outside its dark cave, i.e. "maha" in Arabic, and "mafia" in Italian.

La quota di legittima è non solo un'usanza barbara, denigrante il principio stesso di proprietà e libertà dell'individuo, bensì anche un fattore di dissuasione dal fare testamento.

The reserved portion – "legittima" in Italian testamentary law - is not only a barbaric custom, derogatory of the very principle of property and freedom of the individual, but also a factor of deterrence from making a last will.

Non a caso gli integralisti islamici professano l'infibulazione per le donne, come a voler demonizzare il piacere femminile e nella subcultura italo-mafiosa, la donna ha un ruolo marginale, nel quale però ella si è perfettamente adattata, evoluta ed ambientata, per via del naturale istinto di sopravvivenza ed a fronte delle violenze subite nei propri confronti dalla mentalità maniaco-possessiva del maschio arabo-mafioso.

It's no coincidence Islamic fundamentalists profess infibulation for women, as to demonize female pleasure and, in the Italian-mafia subculture, women have a marginal role, in which they have perfectly adapted, evolved and familiarized, due to the natural survival instinct, in the face of the violence they suffered by maniac-possessive mentality of Arab-like, mafioso males.

Qualora fosse oggettivamente giunto il momento di concludere che l'esperienza di una Repubblica Italiana parlamentare si sia risolta in maniera fallimentare, allora una Repubblica Italiana presidenziale non sarebbe da sottovalutare affatto.

If it was time to objectively conclude that Italian parliamentary Republic experience resolved in a failure, an Italian presidential Republic would not have to be underestimated at all.

Come l'Italia riconosce la Repubblica di San Marino, il conflitto israelo-palestinese si potrebbe risolvere in una soluzione con due stati, ove Gaza potrebbe diventare lo Stato indipendente di Palestina. Ciò tenendo fortemente in considerazione la conformazione geopolitica del Medio Oriente, e la diffusione linguistica dell'arabo in genere. Nell'ottica del Medio Oriente nella sua interezza, l'arabo è la lingua più diffusa, ragion per cui la Palestina avrebbe già in partenza un vantaggio nell'area dovuto alla mancanza di barriere linguistiche. L'ebraico, d'altro canto, è una lingua parlata solo da una minoranza delle popolazioni del Medio Oriente e ciò è sufficiente a considerarla maggiormente a rischio e quindi necessita di maggiore protezione.

As Italy recognizes the Republic of San Marino, the Israeli-Palestinian conflict could be solved with a two States solution, whereas Gaza became the independent State of Palestine. Such solution strongly takes into consideration the Middle East geopolitical scenario and the diffusion of the Arabic language in general. From the perspective of the Middle East as a region, Arabic is the most widely spoken language, therefore Palestine would already have an advantage in the area, due to the lack of linguistic barriers. Hebrew, on the other hand, is a language spoken only by a minority of the population of the Middle East, and this is enough to consider it more at risk, therefore requiring greater protection.

Non desidero più essere cittadino italiano, in quanto mi sento americano, non italiano. Inoltre, non sento ci sia nulla che possa fare per contribuire positivamente alla crescita ed al processo di maturazione dell'Italia in questo frangente storico. Infatti, qualsiasi cosa faccia o dica sembra crei solo odio e disprezzo nei miei confronti.

I no longer want the Italian citizenship, as I feel American, not Italian. Furthermore, I do not feel there is anything I can do to positively contribute to the development and maturity process of Italy, at this time in history. In fact, everything I do or say seems to create only hate and hatred toward me.

L'imagismo è in letteratura come l'impressionismo in pittura.

Imagism is in literature like impressionism in painting.

Il Castello longobardo di Venafro, o Castel Pandone, costruito nel XV secolo ricorda fortemente le Guerra delle Due Rose in Inghilterra (1455–1485), combattuta tra i Lancaster e gli York. Infatti, Castel Pandone è di color rosa, mentre i simboli dei Lancaster e degli York erano rispettivamente una rosa rossa ed una bianca. In un certo senso, il rosa non è altro che l'unione di una rosa rossa ed una bianca.

The Lombard castle of Venafro, aka Castel Pandone, built in the 15th century, strongly recalls the British Wars of the Roses (1455–1485) between the Lancasterians and Yorkists. In fact, Castel Pandone is pink in color, whereas the symbols of the Lancastrians and Yorkists were a red and a white rose respectively. In a way, a pink rose is nothing but the union of red and white roses.

Oltre al color rosa del Catello longobardo di Venafro, che si riferisce agli episodi inglesi della Guerra delle Due Rose, l'iscrizione in pietra ivi rinvenuta e riportante il numero di morti durante la locale pandemia, anch'essa ricorda la storia britannica. Infatti, fu solo durante la Guerra dei Cent'anni tra Inghilterra e Francia, conclusasi con la vittoria di Santa Giovanna d'Arco, che la Morte nera ha cominciato a devastare l'Europa. Secondo le date, ci sono voluti circa due secoli prima che la peste raggiungesse Venafro, mentre l'Inghilterra stava vivendo l'ascesa al trono dei Tudor con Enrico VIII, subito dopo la Guerra delle Due Rose. Forse, la scelta del colore rosa voleva rappresentare proprio la neutralità di Venafro negli episodi che videro contrapposti Enrico VIII e Papa Giulio II.

Other than the pink theme of Venafro's Lombard castle referring to the English episodes of the War of the Roses; the inscription in stone there found, reporting the number of deaths during the local pandemic, also recalls British history as well. In fact, it was just during the Hundred Years' War between England and France, ended with the victory of St. Joan of Arc, that the Black Death began to ravage Europe. According to the dates, it took about two centuries for the plague to reach Venafro, while England was experiencing the escalation of the Tudors and Henry VIII, right after the War of the Roses. Perhaps, the pink color wanted to represent Venafro's neutral role in the episodes which contrasted Henry VIII and Pope Julius II.

Letter to Alex John, Venafro, June 6, 2013

Dear Alex,

On 1/11/11 I was on your show, and talked to you from Venafro (Italy.) I told you Italians were not, or did not seem very aware of the NWO. We also talked about the fact that Italy has a high rate of tax evasion, and an overall black cash-market.

As of today, I regret informing you that, in all actuality, Italians are simply playing dumb. They are very aware of all is going on, and always have been. Their indifference simply means they support the opposite of the NWO, which is an Arab alternative model.

As well renowned, majority of Italians are of Arab, Middle Eastern descent. Despite they distance themselves from Arabs, in all reality they secretly support and encourage the Arab way of living, whereas I can assure you that what they are plotting is much worse than the NWO.

Italian inconclusive political talk and rhetoric, despite the horrible economical situation they got themselves in, by mean of corruption and mafia infiltrations into political institutions is just the proof of their real stand.

Ironically speaking, as Martin Luther King, Jr. said, "The hottest place in hell is reserved for those who remain neutral in times of great moral conflict." In Italy, the same saying states, "Those who remain silent, give their consent." However, Italians are not giving their consent to the NWO, bur rather to caos, illegality, and their Arab-mafia subculture, which has nothing to do with the real Italian heritage and culture.

By the way, mafia is terrorism, in the sense that when someone tries to impose his (women don't count in the Arab-mafia culture) domain and willing above the law, then conflict is inevitable. I am afraid this is what the NWO is rally about, as I have come to learn it over time.

I even sued the governor of the Bank of Italy (Mario Draghi) for usury, and also ran for major of my town (Venafro.) Yet, not a single citizen answered my call. Italian silence is well known as "omertà" or code of silence. It has its roots in the Arab word "maha," where the later Italianized term "mafia" derives from. Not by chance "Maha" means cave or hidden grotto.

I am convinced one cannot fight change, but can only contain and better canalize it. Therefore, between the NWO and an Arab-like, mafia domination, I'll rather choose the NWO.

Sincerely,

Rinaldo Pilla

English erotic literature

I would like to have my dick sucked while writing a poem, as I am sure Ovid and Horace used to do in Venafro back at his time.

Summer is coming, and I see nice pretty students of the classical lyceum here in Venafro showing off parts of their bodies.

Being very careful not to look at the very young ones, only the adult students attract my look and fantasy, wondering if they can feel my desire.

I seat on the rock right outside the cathedral, waiting for someone to ask what I am writing or doing there, almost all day long.

I also hope the priest, Father Salvatore, won't start wondering what I do here. Nevertheless, I am in reality just writing.

However, the genitors at the lyceum, just in front of the cathedral, have already called the police to come and check on me. However, I was only reading.

The days go by, and I start thinking I'd like to be a gigolo, especially because the economy is really bad now, and I need money really bad.

Staying at home is almost impossible; as I am afraid my mother is starting to lose her mental lucidity, and acting as if she were a pagan zengar.

She constantly gets in the way, as if she was trying to catch me masturbating, or making noises right while I am falling asleep, as to interfere or enter my dreams.

Furthermore, I have literally divorced from all my relatives, not only my family. I no longer speak to my mother, my uncles, ants or cousins, if not to my brother and father.

Our cultural background is too different and not compatible at all. I don't mind seeing them around, but definitely I do not want anything to do with them.

Life is rough these days, and the fact I haven't had sex in five years does not make it any easier. On top of that, I got a wart right on my foreskin, from masturbating, which I just had removed.

The conditions are so bad, I have nothing left to do, but trying to sell my dick and my sperm. I am aware of diseases, but what else could I do? I tried them all.

I have even thought asking Father Salvatore if it was possible to rent a small flat at the cathedral, or any other church, in order to get out of the house where I currently live, with my family.

However, the thought of having to pay for a new electric and gas contract, on top of paying for the utilities makes me wonder if that were really a good idea.

At home, at least, I am granted food by law, therefore my mother cannot refuse to feed me. They pay for the electricity, gas and hot water. On top of it, my father also pays for the phone line and the internet.

My mom, especially, acts and seems as if she were pagan rather than Christian, as typical of the mafia culture, which unfortunately is pretty diffused in the entire territory of Southern Italy.

They refuse and reject logic, despite going to the doctor when strictly necessary, and think that truth speaks to them through the sounds of animals, or the appearance of insects, or even through a fire.

Not that she may be any upper class mafia affiliate, just the visible result of the effects of a mafia culture visible among the most vulnerable members of society, who are dominated by fear and intimidation.

The Church does its best to contrast such a phenomenon, despite at first site my mother may seem a perfect church fellow, attending Mass at least once a week, just like most Italians.

However, despite receiving a pension, like many others, she is so afraid of being stalked to death that she stalks younger people in order to scare them away, not even understanding those are the ones paying for her pension.

Her most refined concept of economics is spending as little as possible of her pension, while saving most of it at the bank as if that way the bank will protect her being stalked and stressed to death.

It is because of this very and totally wrong economical concept that I find myself in the middle of the street right now, without a penny in my wallet, and looking for sex in order to make some money.

And there is nothing I can do if that's the way poets do. I only hope not to end up like Ovid, who before me set right here in Venafro, wrote about the sexual costumes of his time, then was sent to the Black Sea on exile.

Even more intriguing is that this day of early May, I am still writing on the rock, with my back lain against the granite column outside the cathedral, right in front of an old stone plaque with inscribed the name of Cicero.

The plaque reads, "M Popilli C, Ciceronis Vivus, Sibi Et Suis Fecit Et..," and something else I cannot decipher. Cicero was murdered by C. Popilius Laenas, who decapitated him in Formia, while trying to escape to Macedonia.

This very small, round rock seemed to me as extraordinary charged with energy, due to its historical location, placed between Pontius Pilate's home, and a memorial plaque to Cicero's death.

So far however, it has proved of very little financial luck to me, despite being a great source of inspiration. Cars drive by, but drivers are disrespectful of traffic laws, constantly honking the horn as if trying to disturb me.

I am afraid the local population is extremely bothered by my presence, despite they can see I am obviously only writing, and doing nothing else. Perhaps they are only disturbed by the fact I write and think in English.

In fact, it has gotten pretty clear they can pick on my thoughts, due to the fact my brain is pretty powerful compared to theirs, therefore they don't like the electromagnetic waves I irradiate my surroundings with.

They reject telepathy, just like it may have happened at the time of the Homo sapiens and the Neanderthals. In this case, they seem to me just like the Neanderthals, who try fighting telepathy with noise.

They are even opening a new sandwich bar, right by the lyceum, on the Pilate's block, called Alexander, which reminds me of Alexander the great, and the fact that I need money in order to survive.

At the horizon I only see the lyceum, the Saint Mary of Carmel church, Pilate's block, and the old Venafro, all surrounded by mountains. Personally I think that a few skyscrapers would look nice, and even add a touch of modern.

I just spoke to an English teacher of the lyceum, who was also complaining about the economical situation, despite being lucky to have a job. Globalization has been a century old process now, with two wars and great fear of a third one.

What I am witnessing under my eyes is the transition and the revelation of the New World Order, as the beginning of a new era, just as it has many times happened before, from the classic age to romanticism, to the post WWII period.

There is no much one can really do as change is inevitable, despite all can contribute their own ways, perhaps even just by writing a book or trying to adjust, first mentally, then hopefully also socially.

In a way, the technological evolution has played an important role into this transformation of the world, first by changing the costumes and working habits, then by breaking all previous barriers and possibilities.

Darwin may have been right saying that is not the strongest, nor the most intelligent, but the most adaptable that has the greatest possibilities of survival on an evolutionary plane.

Adaptation and acceptance of reality is what has led me here on this rock today, looking for ways to get by until better times kick in, and I'll no longer have to sit in the street.

I surely do not count on my books to make a living, as an artist has never fed himself or herself with art, which usually becomes such only after the death of the artist, so it has always been.

Unfortunately the situation for me is pretty clear. If I don't fuck I don't make money, and I don't make money I don't eat. And, I really would like to leave my family's house to live on my own.

What is for sure is that I regret having moved back to Italy, as my life was much better in the US, in terms of personal freedoms, mental health and social acceptance; without even mentioning independence.

Thinking about the past however won't help me, as I am now stuck right here, even though I cannot turn into a primitive as well, and only to please the locals and their mafia culture, which has turned them into ghettoes.

By the way, noticing a hawk flying in the sky once made me think that perhaps those ancient representations of flying objects, often referred to as UFOs, were nothing more than symbols of such animals they were wishing to ride one day.

I am not even sure I'll ever be able to find any local customers here in Venafro, despite I'm willing to inseminate women for only ten euros, and then they can give their baby up to adoption for twenty thousand, which these days is a real deal.

I woke up this morning thinking that getting a wart on my foreskin from masturbation was quite bizarre, considering it never happened when I used to have sex regularly. I guess petting is much better than masturbating, as it prevents from getting warts.

That made me remember when I was about twelve, and used to play doctor with a cousin of mine, which basically consisted in nothing more than petting, without any kind of genital contact or anything else.

At the point where I am at, I'd rather do some petting than keep masturbating, even if it only had to consist in rubbing my dick, in my underwear, against the mattress, given that at thirty-six, I still gotta watch out for my nagging mother.

Thank God I was able to freely explore my own sexuality while living in America, otherwise I don't know what kind of frustrated and repressed man I would be by now, if I stayed in Italy all my life.

Italians don't seem to understand at all the concept of privacy, self determination, and right to procreation. This is only because of the Arab cultural heritage, which gave birth to mafia, from the Arab word "maha," meaning cave, therefore darkness.

Despite liberation happened more or less seventy years ago, Italians are still trapped by those Arab stereotypes, and fatigue to find their way out to a true personal and individual freedom, which is enjoyable in America and most of Europe.

This sexual alienation seems to be driving and influencing their economical relations and relationships as well, and even manifests itself at higher political levels, with the inability to take the necessary measures and changes to solve the problems of the Nation.

The current Italian popular culture has not matured rapidly enough, compared to the technological revolution and international political resolutions, which have not been waiting for the common people to fully digest the complexity of the issues.

In fact, I miss American women a lot these days, much more mature than Italian ones, under certain aspects. I think it will be almost impossible for me to find an Italian mate, mostly because of the negative example of my own mother.

I wouldn't want to become old with a woman like her, and I'm afraid that's how most Italian women turn with age. As far as being a gigolo, that doesn't really matter, as biologically we all fuck alike.

Perhaps Venafro is too much of a closed culture, and local women are afraid to stop by a gigolo, because of the fear of being judged by others. Hopefully I'll have some luck with tourists or foreigners, much more uninhibited.

I don't even like the excess of the typical Italian family culture, which is too constrictive in some ways, and proves weak in times of crisis like this, where a stronger sense of community, not family, is much more desirable.

It's almost as if Italians would like the world to adapt to them, rather than they having to adapt to the world. And, I am afraid this is also true in the Arab and African regions as well, for obvious geographical locations.

In a way, Italy's modern situation resembles ancient Rome, whereas the military was successful, yet the politics confused and conspiratorial, to the point military leaders became emperors, signing the decline of the republic, and the birth of false idols.

Under many aspects, the US also resembles Rome, therefore Italy, especially after its liberation following WWII. The US republic however is more mature than Italy's, and perhaps better balanced between political and military powers.

Over here, people refer to vaginas as butterflies. I have only now understood why, as one just softly posed on my finger. I noticed its slightly closed wings, and a hairy abdomen, with a straw beak inspecting my skin.

In all reality, that's just what a vagina looks like, closed at first, waiting to be sensed with a stick, but only after it has warmed up and opened her labia to let you in, free to drink her nectar, she kindly gives.

After a brief nap, I noticed the granite column was no longer providing shade, so I had to move in order to find some rest, with only men driving by, and no signs of fun time, or any buck from anyone willing to join in my afternoon siesta.

Outside the cathedral is pretty dirty though, with plastic glasses in the yard, beer cans, and empty pack of cigarettes. One man just stopped by to cut the grass this morning, and in it was a great mess of garbage.

No wonder I get no customers, the parking lot is empty, as I guess it's Saturday afternoon, and everybody may be napping at home in their beds, not like me, on a rock, despite I should go lain on the lawn.

There are nice lawns right behind the cathedral, among the olive trees, which are actually part of a regional park, and quite honestly, they inspire a lot of good sex, watching out for the scouts, who are just in front of Pilate's villa.

I wouldn't actually mind going all the way up to the Norman tower either, recently restored, with a nice balcony, like the one of Romeo and Juliet. I am sure a horny babe would have lots of fun, with the altitude and the view.

Just a while ago, Father Salvatore passed by in his car, and stopped at the scouts, where I guess they're having a meeting of some kind. That makes me actually think that my mother used to say she always wanted to become a nun.

I am afraid her horrible demeanor developed over time may depend by the fact she rejected her vocation, and married my father instead. She shouldn't have had me; therefore I am assuming our bad relation is the result of such decision.

All this experience upon my return to Italy made me realize that platonic love is now obsolete and out of fashion, whereas Christian love is much broader and encompassing, as it also allows for what is generally considered platonic love.

Wondering why so many churches in Venafro, other than being Pontius Pilate's city, it is also clear that the Church is at the center of the community, and not only architectonically at the center of every square.

The fact that faith based communities have scientifically proven higher rates of longevity among their members is also nowadays advertised in Iowa, through the Blue Zones projects, which I would implement in Venafro as well.

This morning I ate an avocado fruit, as I was accustomed to, back in the US. I saved the seed, and once over here at the cathedral, I planted it, despite I am well aware of its little possibilities of success.

Actually, in the past two years I have been living here in Venafro, I have been experiencing a lot with botanic. I planted some figs and hazelnut on the Winterline, together with some pines and a mixture of other seeds.

I have also successfully planted a eucalypt tree, which survived its first winter in Venafro, after having freed five little lab mice, wondering if I'll ever see them again. I also threw some hemp seeds across Mount Holy Cross, and some Venus' flytrap.

On top of that, I even planted some kiwi fruit, always along the Winterline, some lavender, strawberries, leontopodium, forget-me-not, an agave by the Norman tower, and many other kind of flowers, wondering if I would ever see their flowers.

Venafro has a very mild weather, whereas winters are chill, but it rarely snows in the city, despite it is possible to see snow on the surrounding mountains till May. While summer is pleasantly hot, sometimes humid, sometimes dry.

Swallows seem to love it here in springtime, where they usually arrive in May, which usually is characterized by a nice breeze, some rainy days, and some hotter ones, announcing the upcoming summer, to bring its full heat.

I am not sure how much climate change may have affected Venafro, as my youth memories are about vein, and NATO military programs to contrast Earth's overheating are in place over here too, not just in the US. Perhaps they really are necessary and inevitable.

It is funny how looking at the sky one could symbolize the daily life. As soon as a buzzard leaves its nest to fly in the sky, right away crows appear to disturb it. That's just like in life, when one leaves his home finds lots of danger, and may never find the way back.

The same is for hawks and eagles, and when times get rough, the Church rejects violence. However, the military starts to combat to clean the mess, as too many crows are not good for human life, and prayers alone cannot disperse them.

So my days go by in Venafro, whereas the locals fatigue to realize the situation, yet too cowards to speak up, or even help their priest, who left alone has very little power against the upcoming risks, and I cannot but seat and watch.

Personally, just like the Pope at the Vatican farm in Castel Gandolfo, I would not allow for crows in the city, especially by children, as their natural predatory and opportunistic instinct could be manipulated by bad people, and domesticated to stalk others.

This however, only twenty years ago would have never been allowed, if not for the decay and decadence the economical crisis has brought with it, making it almost impossible to patrol the city, and avoiding crime and mafia taking over.

After all, this is nothing new, especially in Italy, so badly influenced by this disgusting Arab sub-culture, which still permeates it, especially in the South. As usual, this will conclude with some social frictions, and the reestablishment of law and order.

In fact, I had now many times said that the New World Order is nothing more than the world without mafia or any other terrorist culture. I know this will happen, but I don't know what the costs of this universal transformation will be.

I feel very privileged for being able to write right here by the cathedral of Venafro, where there are pictures and frescoes with Jewish inscriptions, as to testify my own heritage, a Christian Jew always loyal to Christ, and His Church.

I feel at home over Pilate's Villa, and noticing the facade of the cathedral with its rose window on top, I cannot but think of a vagina, waiting for some light to shine through its hole, all the way into the uterus.

The church inside is just like the representation of the uterus. After all, with all its elements waiting to come alive, day after day, under the light shining through the rose window, just like a uterus awaits fecundation by sperm.

No doubts sexual symbolism has driven human development since the time of the very first appearance of permanent settlements in Mesopotamia and Egypt, but even before, during the Paleo and Neolithic, with representations of vulvas and phalli.

After all, without sex there would be no procreation, therefore disobeying God's own commandment to reproduce and multiply in order to prepare the planet for His kingdom and His final and ultimate revelation.

I sense this time has almost come, despite I cannot know for sure if this very same feeling is common across mankind at one point in every human being's developmental progression, or even across different historical periods.

Today I feel like "the thinker," as often portrayed in many sculptures, and even present in San Francisco, due to the fact I sit here by the column, often getting lost into my thoughts in search for inspiration, while focusing on the blue, immense horizon.

I have also noticed that one of people's many concerns is the fear of death, which constantly puts them in a very depressed and resigned state of mind. This also is due to the Afro-Arabic mafia culture, evolved from the cult of Set, core of the strategy of terror.

In a way, this is exactly what the Church fights, following Christ's own teachings, and believing on Christian's final victory over such rudimental and in vane culture of death, embraced by mafia and its affiliates.

It is this fear of death and lack of faith to be causing the majority of the world's social and economical crisis, therefore behind all wars fought in the name of this creed among lost souls, who are walking dead, and the people of faith.

For a Christian, the Children of Israel are exactly that, i.e. those who have found God on this planet, versus those who have always rejected and denied Him, believing in false gods or philosophies, which inevitably eat them alive.

What is even more interesting, is the fact these inferior beings can nothing against the Children of Israel, absolutely nothing. They can only disturb those who are asleep, therefore unaware of either calls, i.e. the blessed ignorant.

As a matter of fact, the statue of the sitting bishop, Pietro of Ravenna, on the lateral bell tower of the cathedral clearly shows the man holding a stick on his left hand, which makes me think of an early educator, when Catholicism was taught outside the church.

The statue does not give me the impression the bishop used the stick to hit the children, rather using it to hit a tree, a rock or even the ground to make a sound, in order to keep the children paying attention and alert, or even draw with it.

In a way, a lay person may use his dick just like a stick; therefore that unconscious gesture resembles an intimate bedroom foreplay moment, when couples give each other love and kindness, as an act of maximum attention to one another.

After all, that's what sex is. The time two lovers find for themselves, as a moment of alienation from the surrounding world, finding refuge in the grace of God, serenity, warmth and tranquility of a beloved soul mate, recreating that original tie.

Actually, another thing I have noticed among Italians is their strict similarity, result of century old interbreeding, therefore creating a pretty unique genetical footprint, carrying with it several genetic anomalies, due to the lack of gene renewal.

This phenomenon is particularly noticeable by the very high concentration of bald men and weak denture genetic makeup of Italians, which does not occur in the US for example, due to the much diffused intermixing, despite I refuse interracial unions.

Basically, it is possible to say that Italians are so genetically related that they are all brothers and sisters committing incest unintentionally by keep marrying among them, and also creating lower IQ offspring over time.

This phenomenon is also responsible for the diffused and widespread mafia culture and economical collapse, due to Italy's inability to reject communist influences and philosophies, with the subsequent stagnation of its society as well as its gene pool.

Historically, this is also noticeable by the behavior of Italian women, who don't seem liking African men much, as unconsciously they are aware that's where all these problems originate from. However, only time will tell if I am right or not.

By the way, having all this time now, I have also been thinking about some of my previous studies and writings, particularly about the opium fields in Afghanistan, allegedly guarded by US troops. My father uses metamorphine, therefore those soldiers are actually helping rather than trafficking.

The same goes for my criticism toward Zionist policies, which I came to realize as legitimate, due to the State of Israel endless war against the very same barbarian culture, otherwise known as mafia in Italy. Nevertheless, mafia is nothing more than a terrorist organization.

Being by Pilate's home, in search for inspiration, made me also realize that Christ never stopped teaching, even while dying on the cross. In fact, had he not said, "Father, why did you abandon me?" we would have never understood the "dubito ergo sum."

Today I am at the hospital in Isernia, as my father has to undergo a little surgery. Upon my arrival, I noticed some people standing right outside the chapel where they place the patients who pass away while hospitalized, awaiting for a funeral.

Contrary to the US, I noticed sad faces, and this made me think that perhaps, if they had known catechism a little better, they would probably have had beer instead and chatted to mourn their dead a little bit better.

In fact, just as the Shroud of Turin, which is the negative of Christ, so afterlife is the negative of this earthly reality. This means the two things are two aspects of the same reality. And, also for this teaching one has to thank Christ.

Actually, I remember when I was about eight or nine years old, and came to Venafro with my parents to visit my grandparents. My cousins convinced me to come right here at the cathedral, as Father Salvatore, a very young priest at the time, was confessing there.

I was used to my priest of the time, Father Antonio, in Cicciano near Naples, where I moved during my elementary school period, from Turin. Anyway, Father Salvatore confessed me, and asked I preyed the Act of Contrition, which I didn't know. So, I ran away from him outside the cathedral, right where I stand now.

It has been over a month now, since I last wrote anything in addition to this narration. I had to take care of my father, who got bladder surgery done at the hospital in Isernia, about twenty minutes away from Venafro. His recovery has been quite slow so far.

I haven't been by the Cathedral in Venafro for a long time, if not to stop by and leave some money under its door, for an offer. At the hospital I was very pleased to have pretty nice nurses walking around almost all day long, with their see-through white pants.

With great pleasure and excitement, while my dad was hospitalized, one evening I was even able to sneak a peak at the nurse's office, seeing a beautiful brunette nurse by the name of Gabriella or Graziella straighten out her black panty, which gave me a hard on.

Eventually, I ended up bringing my Playboy magazine at the hospital as well, just to entertain the other man who was hospitalized next to my father, in the same room. He had never seen a US version of Playboy, but was very pleased to take a look.

As far as having sex, unfortunately for me, I haven't seen a pussy what's so ever! I am trying to embark onboard of a cruise ship, for work. I am really broke, and my teaching job has almost come to an end. There is a possibility to sail away for five months.

Working on a cruise ship will not get me off below the poverty line, to which I have been accustomed living for decades now, but will surely provide some relief to my personal finances. On top of that, it may be the only way I could get laid over here in Italy.

Actually, just a few days ago I went to the U.S. Consulate in Naples, in order to get my last will notarized by the Consul. Just outside the building, there was a group of five or six smoking hot, blond tourists, whom I asked to take me away with them, yet unsuccessfully.

After all the disgusting fights and aggression with my mother's family, especially one of his brothers, which forced me to report him and his aggression to the local Police, I decided I no longer want to be an Italian citizen, as I feel American, not Italian.

I have realized how culturally different Italians are, and I have nothing in common with them. Most likely, that is also the reason why I don't seem able to find a girlfriend over here in Italy. Perhaps, it's better that way, otherwise I'll have never realized all that.

Moreover, I don't think there is anything else I can do to help them. Italians are very stupid and ignorant, to the point they will soon realize the bubble they live in is going to implode. At that point I am not sure what they will do or how they'll handle reality.

Moreover, I don't think there is anything else I can do to help them. Italians are very stupid and ignorant, to the point they will soon realize the bubble they live in is going to implode. At that point I am not sure what they will do or how they'll handle reality.

The 2013 elections for the Major of Venafro are over, and I didn't even have a chance to run, as nobody in the entire city contacted me, talked to me or even asked me what my intentions and plans were. Local people have only harassed, ignored and stalked me.

The funniest thing is that I was treated the worst by my mother's own relatives, which happen to be my neighbors as well. I am really ashamed of all of them; to the point I no longer talk or look for them. Perhaps, that' just another reason why I wan to embark.

Italians have their sneaky way of stalking others pretending they are doing something or talking to someone else right when you are walking by or around, and coincidentally what they are saying is related to something you are doing in that moment or somehow related.

In a way they think to be able to threaten or scare you by trying to make you understand they control everything you do in your life, as to have full control over your own life and persona. Actually, this is nothing more the so called "mafia method."

Since the word mafia derives from the Arabic "maha," meaning dark cave, I guess this method of stalking people only works among troglodytes, or cavemen like my mothers' relatives. Nevertheless, it's illegal behavior and the root cause of all Italian troubles.

It is also possible women do not dare talking to me or approaching me because they are threatened the same way by the very same people who try scarring me, in order to keep them away from me, as to isolate me. Isolating me would make me more vulnerable.

This is one reason why I think American women are superior to Italian women in general. An American woman will never live up to this bullshit these Arab-like, Italian mafia men get by with over here. They are extinct, walking dead or even zombies.

To tell the truth, I really miss the presence of an American woman in my life. Italian women are just like Arab women themselves by majority, despite the fact they don't wear a burka. After all, they breed these stupid men, not me.

To be honest, I also must admit that, had it not been for my return to Italy, I would have never fully realized the issues President George Bush was dealing with, while I was living in the United States. In fact, after living here, I have realized what he was talking about.

Ironically speaking, now that I live in Italy, I would like to return to the U.S., despite I am glad I got a chance to enjoy my father, and assist him in this delicate moment of his life. I guess one cannot have everything in life, or at least not at once.

I have also been developing a certain constant, recurrent thought in my mind lately. In fact, I am not afraid of saying I would like to date Former President George W. Bush's daughter, Barbara Bush. I think it could be fun having George Bush as father in law.

Now, that doesn't mean I'd like to date Barbara Bush only because of her father. She looks pretty and sexy on the Media; despite I have never seen her in person. Also, she is pretty committed to humanitarian and health causes around the world.

The few times I have watched her appearances on TV, promoting her humanitarian affiliation and talking about the projects she is involved with, I have had a very good impression of her intentions, ambitions, and overall intellectual affinity with me.

I mean, I was being cheese there, as I have offended Mr. Bush enough previously, to the point I no longer want to take a chance at looking as if I am now starting to stalk his daughter as well. Barbara Bush is a woman of great intellectual gauge.

However, if I keep dreaming about all the women I cannot have, I'll really never fuck again for the rest of my life. I have been contemplating prostitutes as well, but due to my financial condition, I cannot even afford one, especially for the length of time needed.

I guess my gigolo attempt plunged as well, and I cannot even change town or move elsewhere for good as I do not want to leave my dad alone for too long. Embarking for five months seems the best option at the moment, despite still not sure.

It will give me the time needed for myself, as I have not taken a vacation in four years now, nor I have left Italy ever since. I feel drained by my mother's relatives, and the overall familial situation, whereas she still rejects hiring a caretaker for my dad.

I don't understand their concerns, as they could afford one easily. They are just mean in general, meaning not only selfish, but penny-pinching as well. They still believe money can save their lives, as if it was a shield against death or mafia persecutions.

The only other explanation for her behaviors is that she's lesbian, unconsciously; and she refuses even to consider such possibility. I am afraid a great number of people, especially in Southern Italy, are sexually repressed gays who do anything to hide it.

I am afraid acceptance of one's own sexuality plays a fundamental role in the development of one's psyche and overall psychological and emotional balance as well. Understanding who we are, sexually at first, may even help us live our dreams more freely.

If that was the case, I could testify that there is nothing worst for a man than being born by a lesbian mother who repressed her real sexuality to the point of ruining not only her own existence and that of her spouse, but even that of her own children.

Perhaps this very last statement would also explain the reason why the Church promotes such strict policies in regard of the importance and sacrament of marriage between a man and a woman, and is though on gays as their unions are not aimed to procreation.

Personally, I am not able to distinguish a gay from a straight person, unless he or she openly lives his or her sexuality without any possibility of misunderstanding. It is also very possible repressed gays may be easy targets of illicit criminal organization due to their weak psyche.

While living in the U.S., I was friend with many gay people, and never had any kind of problem interacting or spending time with them. Actually, the very opposite it true, i.e. I always felt very comfortable accepting other people's sexuality and sexual preferences.

One night, while in Des Moines, I even had sex in the same house with my girlfriend, while sleeping overnight over at a gay couple's house. We were under the same roof, yet sleeping in two separate bedrooms, each freely loving one another.

Italy is still miles far away from allowing such forms of personal independence and freedom, despite the law already grants everyone the right to her or his own sexual identity and preferences. Being able to freely express one's sexual orientation is vital.

I have actually come to understand that, outside from a professional environment, when one does not clearly defines his or her own sexual orientation, it is better to be precautious, considering them repressed gays, for the wellbeing of a straight person.

I liked being picked up by girls in America, as when a girl comes to you is because she is pretty confident of her own sexuality, to the point she has no problems living her condition and trying to satisfy her sexual instinct. Over here, I haven't had any of that.

I have never had sex with an Italian woman, and at this point in my life, I do not even regret it. I even slept one night with an Indian (from India) doctor who was working in Iowa City. However, I greatly prefer Caucasian women, especially blonds.

The thing that scares me most about having sex with Italian women is the fact that in case my lover should get pregnant, then I'll have to deal with stupid Italian hereditary laws such as the legitime, i.e. the forced legal share that cannot be disinherited.

Basically, the most Italian women breed and have children with a man only because of the existence of such legal instrument, known as legitime. Now, this is also the case for lesbians for example, who otherwise would rather become nuns.

Perhaps the fact I openly tell this things in public, is also the reason why Italian women avoid me, on top of the fear of being stalked by the mafia cavemen who do anything possible to make me go away; therefore, I must absolutely not find a girlfriend here.

Nevertheless, everything leads me to look back to America, especially when it comes down to women. However, at the moment, the closer I can get to American women is by jerking off at Playboy's Playmates for the month, which I enjoy doing.

So, this is my real situation at the moment. A sick father and a repressed lesbian mother; fucked up, mafia like cultured relatives, and above anything else, without female life companions. I cannot but hope for Hillary Clinton to become President.

I am actually so bothered by my mother's relatives; I now call them the "nigga family." Given that I still strongly foresee a clear link between African voodoo, i.e. a tribal cult, and the Arab-born mafia affiliation. Therefore, they all think to be masters of black magic.

Italian popular culture is still nowadays persuaded by these primitive mentalities and believes, to the point it almost seems impossible the Vatican is actually located in Italy. This culture is also reflected as stereotyping of Italian in general by the Media.

Paradoxically speaking, it's black people who actually end up believing these primitive teachings the most. It is hard to decide who influences whom. Nevertheless, Italian women are trapped in this endless game of constant fight for economical control of the territory.

Nevertheless, I can honestly say that my FBI arrest, including one night in jail at the Scott County Court House and Jail has been very educational for me. In fact, I have been able to verify first hand that justice in Italy does not work at all, assuring no protection what so ever.

Despite all my police reports for stalking and the aggressions by my neighbors and relatives, I have had no real legal protection at all. Furthermore, this negligence of Italian law enforcement officers and judicial system keeps me exposed to abuses and pressures.

Everyday, I have to live by and see abuses and infractions right by my house. These people feel great pleasure and sense of achievement making you feel impotent against them, as if they are superior to the law of the land, and want you to believe they are the law.

This is the kind of Arab-like mafia culture typical of the Arab-mafioso, Italian man, which I am sure, afflicts Italian females as well. Italians live in a ghetto-like cultural marsh they have created themselves, and which they blame for all their problems.

Therefore, Italian women at large are characterized by a self inflicted, victim devious and mischievous mentality. After you have gotten to know them deeply, that's what one finds out about them. That is the reason why I would like to fuck, but rather not.

Once again, this phenomenon may come all the way from the Roman civil law principle of the legitime, which ensures women control over their offspring's hereditary right, by controlling their lives as well, whereas the term Italian "mammoni," or mama's boy.

I guess the lesson I had to learn in life, by virtue of my past experiences, is that at one point one has to choose parts, or where to stand, so to speak. One cannot please everyone, or love everyone the same way. Maturity is the process granted for such purpose.

I have been very critical of many aspects of the international political and social arena, yet always trying to learn as much as possible about the issues I was writing about. While studying, one cannot imagine where such studies will take him or her.

It is true that, in life, one never finish studying or learning. This is also provable from many of my younger writings, when I had little different ideas and takes on many issues, such as economy and wars. Growing up and maturing, I have refined my tastes a lot.

In a way, the very same logic also applies to the taste for women in general. In the end, all I was looking for in life was myself, and now that I know myself a little better, I would like to leave a part of me continuing this journey, by having children.

In fact, another reason why I am very afraid of getting involved with an Italian woman is because of the possibility of procreating. Italian women are very attractive, and I surely wouldn't mind banging a few of them, as I have never had an Italian woman.

However, what really frightens me, other than the legitime, are the worries about having to raise a child born by an Italian woman. The idea just sounds like a nightmare to me, and probably because of my own experiences being born in an Italian family.

As I said before, I do not consider myself Italian, but American. This also means I would have huge difficulties raising a child in Italian as first language, despite the fact I love Italian, as second language though, not my mother tongue or first language.

Being able to speak several languages is pretty common nowadays. However, the more practice a language, the more involved one gets with the culture of that language. It is an inexorable and natural process one cannot avoid. It's like gaining a new personality.

In a way, I feel English has completely taken over my brain, to the point I could easily forget Italian and live harmoniously and comfortably just by speaking English. With age then, one has to start deciding what is really needed in his or her life.

In my case, I have gotten to the conclusion Italian is no longer needed for my well being and overall mental serenity and hygiene. This is perhaps the reason why I still seek American women as life companions; despite I was already divorced once with an American.

I am not saying I would purposely rather forget Italian completely. Nevertheless, I consider it just as a skill to be added to my resume, but nothing more. Probably, this is how diplomatic workers feel, after having served and lived abroad for many years.

The difference, though, is that I am not paid by any Department of State for learning and coexisting with another culture and language. Until I find a way to make such skill profitable, I am destined to a horrible existence of isolation and exclusion.

Ironically speaking, I have gotten to understand that a "New World Order" is a possible remedy to such struggles; not only for those in my very same situation, but also to harmonize the life of all Nations and their people, by improving their coexistence possibilities.

With the worsening of the economical crisis, which I have been predicting to Italians for years now, there is also a strengthening fear for the rise of wars and conflicts. Perhaps, this is another reason why Italian women do not show me any interest or affection.

Ironically speaking, after finding out being of Jewish ancestry, I came to realize that was another possible explanation why women may chose breeding with black people rather than me. I guess a Christian-Jew is just like an African man in some women's mind.

I cannot but keep thinking that interracial breeding is behind many of the problems experienced nowadays, in terms of the offspring they reproduce. In fact, it may be a psychological and biological shock when one is born from two completely different human beings.

In a way, genetical variation is a key factor to evolutionary progress. Yet, too much variation may be the cause of the opposite problem. Unfortunately, humans live on Earth confined by very narrow biological and physical laws, which permit their existence.

This may even be the case why, in the United States, it took several generations before intermixing occurred, even within immigrants of European descendants for example. It is if unconsciously these people knew it would take generations to adapt before interbreeding.

In a way that's exactly how I feel in Italy right now. I was considered an alien in the United States, or legal immigrant coming from Italy. Now, ironically speaking, I feel an alien back in Italy as well, or perhaps it's more like I perceive Italians as aliens to me.

One thing is for sure, that being I have learned very well what cultural shock actually means, and what pains it can cause to one's own psyche. It is not a physical wound one can see or observe yet is a psychological wound needing the same attention.

Accidentally, today, I learned that Ezra Pound was responsible for introducing the Japanese Haiku poetical style in Europe. I was very surprised by that, especially when finding out he was also the one who introduced the term imagism in poetry.

I must admit owing Ezra Pound a lot, and not only for my overall interest in poetry, but as much as in monetary policies as well. However, one thing I am glad I didn't do was making his same mistakes in terms of betraying the U.S. Government.

In fact, despite it was inevitable that the curiosity of my studies would take me very close to many borderline groups of thinkers and their respective philosophies and organizations; I never actively joined any them, but observed only.

I have often gotten much influenced and attached to many of the issues I was studying, as if I had been a secret agent or infiltrator, despite I was not. Sometimes I even felt many of the issues debated and supported against the Government were right.

However, I'll never get tired of repeating it over and over again, I am very glad I never lost all trust in the Government to the point of crossing the no return zone. I would have made the biggest mistake of my life, as I learned that a poet is not a politician.

Ezra Pound was wrong, despite some very good points in denouncing usury, in the sense he failed to get the bigger picture, and the true working mechanism of the monetary apparatus. Modern day bankers are not exactly like the money changers in the temple.

I have tried explaining these in some of my other writings, to make sure future generations didn't think I was a traitor myself, and I am not talking about the U.S. Government. I am not a traitor to myself by having learned more than Ezra Pound did on money.

The monetary equation balancing credit and debt cannot work if the system allows for thefts, such as black market or tax evasion. These factors are what sustain terrorism and mafia worldwide. They are responsible for economical collapses, not banks.

It would be just like trying to constantly inflate a tire, when there is a hole in it. You can blow all the air you want, or pump all the money you want. If that money does not get where it is supposed to, in the end you'll have lost even more energy in the effort.

Ezra Pound supported Mussolini, who, however, lost the war because of his misunderstanding or not full comprehension of monetary policies. I went close to committing the very same mistake; however my constant studying saved me from an unhappy end.

What is even more bizarre, in my opinion, is that Ezra Pound also betrayed Dorothy Shakespeare, his former wife and a British citizen, in order to support Mussolini's cause and lose the war. Their story is very similar to that of Napoleon and his collapse.

As I wrote in my first book, I'll have to live a millennial life in order to find the answers to all my questions. Perhaps, I might even get there by the time I am one hundred fifty, but surely need to be surrounded by many other long-lived people.

In fact, such foresight or long view does not belong, in the animal kingdom, to other creatures whose lifespan is inferior compared to humans. It's like the old saying that in order to understand something one must go thorough and experience it.

Actually, if I really had to define my writing style and what I wished to accomplish with it that would be just imagism. I guess I like thinking of myself of a 21th century imagist poet, whereas with my words I would like to make people dream my scenes.

Outside my own lines, I actually practice the imagism style as a way of leaving, trying to transfer pictures onto others as I talk to them. In a way, that might be considered real telepathy, which I use most of the time. However, that's just a side effect.

While some people have big bellies, I can say to have a big brain. Now, as fat people are usually not charged extra money for occupying extra space, I don't think I should be charged extra money for occupying extra ether with my thoughts.

I cannot help but being telepathically active everywhere I go. Just as a marathon runner is physically more resistant than me, my mind is much superior to many others. With that come a great responsibility and an immense reject by many on my path.

Bottom line, telepathy is real, and I have tried to transfer such very simple truth onto my writings. I am sure new generations are going to use this telepathic potential always more, and I leave up to them to show me where the newly born humans will take us.

Just as Virgil did a few thousand years ago, and many others after him throughout history, I wanted to give humanity a precise picture of the human family as a whole, taken during my lifetime, through my lines. Yet, I never thought I would become a poet.

Many may even wonder if I really wrote more prose rather than poetry as strictly considered. Nevertheless, I consider myself being a true poet, not just a common prose writer. This is especially true due to my huge attempt to transfer images through my lines.

I would be very satisfied if my readers could imagine and visualize in their minds just what I am saying with my words. This would make my lines come alive, just like a movie. In a way, I also aim at influencing my readers with neuro-linguistic programming.

In fact, not only I wanted and aimed at imagism poetical style, but also always kept into consideration the consequences of my words from the prospective of neuro-linguistic programming. Poetry is a very powerful tool to reach and influence the masses.

I hope I used this gift God granted me the best possible way, for the good of humanity, more than my own profit or personal interests. Certainly, I paid a very high price in terms of all the sacrifices I had to go through to fully live my artistic endeavors.

As Italian composer Giuseppe Verdi anticipated in his "Va, pensiero" (The Chorus of the Hebrew Slaves,) from the "Nabucco" (The Chorus of "zingari,") nonsense words in general and talking can recreate Babylon, yet can nothing against the power of thought.

For instance, I must also confess that after having gone through my father's hospitalization, I have come to realize that the medical benefits of radio-frequency identification (RFID) chips far outstand all possible negative fears associated with it.

In fact, most fears associated with such technology are unjustified from a medical prospective. As all things, precaution is legitimate, but trying to criminalize or denigrate innovation, while associating it with overall restrictions of one's rights is terrorism.

Ironically speaking, with age I am not only getting older and more mature, but I am also starting to realize the importance of medical screening and treatments when necessary. Conspiracy theories are fading in front of the ever changing needs of my own aging body.

When I was younger I wasn't even sure about having kids for example; despite now, at age thirty six, my biological clock has finally kicked in. In a way, the same is for a RFID chip, which I now wouldn't mind having implanted in my own subcutaneous layer.

I even wonder if I had an Italian girlfriend right now, would she even understand the kind of questions I ask myself and I reflect upon. This is just another example why American women are perhaps more compatible with me, in terms of common cultural background.

Conspiracies and conspiracy theories can be depressing over time. They can be interesting to study for a while, as the point they try to make requires pretty elaborate thinking. However, in the end, they are just mere fantasy and a source of depression.

In a way, it takes a conspiracy theorist combined with congenital depressive individual to make a so called terrorist. Given that one should focus all the efforts on the present rather than past, as that is the only variable configurable to change the future.

It took me several years of studying to learn all the issues the conspiracy theorists were talking about, and once I finished learning about pretty much everything, I figured it would have been much better, had I focused all my energies on pussy instead.

I cannot help but loving the female body as sublime expression of human beauty. I do appreciate the male body aesthetics; however, its muscle superiority only gives me the impression of being the ultimate proof of male secondary and submissive role on Earth.

In a way one could say males being genetically built to be females' natural slaves. After all, women do not mind being watched with fascinated looks, as long as they are not perverted. Women love to be admired, yet not touched, unless they want to be.

Last night I went out to a club for the first summer evening, and was delighted by all the beautiful girls wearing shorts, miniskirts and sleeveless tops. Many were young, with fantastic velvety skin and beautiful hair. I had to thank summer for such eye delight.

I wish I could have caressed those silky legs with my hands, and kissed them while lifting those skirts to see the undies. Keeping testosterone under control is even harder during summer time, being so highly stimulated all around by feminine grace.

Now more than ever I am really tired of masturbating, and despite it would be impossible for me right now to get my hands on a Playboy's Playmate or Cybergirl, I found it impossible to even think walking down the road and raping and Italian woman.

It is in moments like these I wonder if I should seriously be thinking about paying a prostitute for some sex. I mean, it has been four and a half years since I last had sex now. I don't really want to break any world records of sexual abstinence either.

I don't even want to take into consideration the possibility of becoming a priest either. Actually, I don't even want to prove myself I am not gay, or try to study if my sexual desire and preferences might have changed with abstinence or masturbation.

I just cannot believe it has become so difficult for me getting laid. Perhaps is that I think too much about women as truly equal human beings, therefore I don't look at them as a mere holes to stick my dick in. I love sex, but perhaps I have become too picky.

Without any doubts, living in a small town like Venafro does not help me getting laid either, as I had already explained before. People here are like a closed tribe, whereas a foreigner is not welcomed by other males as he is actually seen as a possible competitor.

What is bizarre is that this mentality still persuades Italy in two thousand thirteen. Once one is faced with such situation, can either leave the tribe or join their customs, becoming one of them, which I really cannot do, as I reject the Arab-mafia culture way too much.

Awaiting with impatience to know if I'll be able to work on a cruise ship or not is horrible at the moment. I am trying to build myself any possible way out of this situation one can possibly imagine. This includes stop warring for my father's health too.

One day, while I was sitting on the stone outside Venafro's Cathedral, someone from the classical high school called the police reporting my presence as suspicious. So, all of sudden two cars stopped by, and an agent asked me to provide him my identity card.

I don't blame the agents for doing their jobs, it's like that this was the kind of overall treatment I have been receiving in Venafro, despite everyone knew I was just writing, and what I was writing about. The officers were even surprised when I showed them my books.

On the other hand, I must also admit that it does not happen everyday, when one finds or sees a poet spending several hours on a stone writing, especially in small communities. I guess, it would have been different, had I been painting the landscape or something else.

It has been very difficult for me to go through all the diffidence I had to face in my life, both in the U.S. and Italy as well. What made it even harder, was the fact I didn't even have a female companion, and all I was left with were solitude and self compassion.

We all have different desires, and they are all equally alike. This is true for love, sex and even last wills. In fact, another lesson I have learned by personal experience is that, in Italy, Americans and Italians cannot live under the same roof, or the same house.

I have come to feel like I have returned back to my biological parents, yet not my physiological ones. It is if I have been adopted and raised by American parents, and now live in completely different, hostile and unwelcoming familial environment.

This is very true especially because of my mother's horrible attitude toward me. She is a villain, and it took me a lot of time to realize her true personality and demeanor. I cannot no longer really stand her, despite I realize she just too ignorant to understand me.

Perhaps this also conditions my relation and attitude toward Italian women in general. However, I really do not want to end having to spend the rest of my life with another woman just like her. I don't mind living in Italy, just not as an Italian, as I don't feel one.

It might even be possible that local women do not approach me not because they are afraid of other men's judgments, but because they are aware of my mother and her sibling's mean personalities, therefore they avoid me as well, still living with her.

The conjunction of economical factors, the overall health status of my father and my business activities related to American interests in Italy, in a town strongly influenced by a mafia culture mixed to communist ideology, may all have contributed to it.

I am stuck, and I don't like it. Sometimes life puts you in situations you had never thought possible, yet once you are forced facing them, your attitude toward life itself cannot but change drastically. All your beliefs vanish, and everything is to be rewritten.

Many may succumb in such situations, and I am not kidding. It's a psychological odyssey what I am going through right now. Sometimes I don't even know how I am able to handle or manage this situation. Nevertheless, my positive attitude keeps me alive.

Another bizarre aspect of my life has been that, several times, I felt in danger for my safety. This is the reason why I wanted to write as much as possible, also in terms of the people I met along the way, just in case something bad would have happened.

Only now I am realizing that writing the names of my exes for example, might not have been a gentleman act itself. However, I have often wondered if they approached me more as spies, rather than lovers. At this point in life I don't even want to know.

I think it would even be possible that Italian mafia always followed my moves while living the U.S., in order to control and eventually take over my wine business for example. They might have been able to do that by contacting local criminals in Davenport.

If that were the case, I would say to be very lucky being alive and able to add these thoughts to my personal story. In fact, I lived in times when terrorism was a real treat to many Nations worldwide. The Government may even have thought I was a mobster.

It is also for such a reason, being my desire to prove my innocence and distance from any kind of criminal organization and affiliates, that I decided to write a last will with U.S. Federal Government as beneficiary of all my possessions and anything else applicable.

In a way, all I really want at this point in my life is just a new life. But, above anything else, I no longer want to have anything to do with the people who, in a way or another, have been part of my previous life. I know is difficult, especially because I love my dad.

I wish nobody to be in the situation of having to chose if taking care of his or her own ill father, or to pretend he does not exist, and move on with their lives, leaving everything else to chance and destiny. I also have almost no collaboration by the police.

It is in this very moment that I miss having a woman around me the most. I understand how no woman may ever want to be dealing with the situation I am in right now, or she will be more like a Virgin Mary than just a simple member of the other sex.

A woman is also the best medicine for stress and depression in my opinion. She may cause another kind of stress, but wouldn't surely be the kind can actually destroy a person physically, morally, psychologically and emotionally all at the same time.

In a way, right now I feel so alone as if my life did not matter to anyone on the planet. Fortunately enough though, my psyche is very strong and solid, to the point I can write about my feelings without even considering the possibility of depression.

Through this experience I have also come to understand how many teenagers may feel when they decide to commit some very stupid actions, as a consequence of this very same feeling, which in their case takes over and creates such a depressive state to commit suicide.

Of course, for them the problems faced might be completely different, yet creating the same feelings and bad moods which I am exposed to right now as well. I would like them to take a little bit of my spirit in order to overcome such states of mind.

Some may even need medical treatment, due to some chemical element deficiency. At least, I was lucky enough not to have that problem. I would have never been able to withstand all the pressure I am right now if I had had such deficiencies too.

I think that Italy's biggest problem is that Italians are very incompetent when it comes down to dealing with money. In a way, had I not lived in the United States, I'd have been just like them. Thank God I am not! Once again, ignorance is man's greatest fault.

This is also another fundamental aspect dictating Italy's enslavement to mafia. In fact, when the economical system is concentrated in few incompetent hands, all others are subject to such individuals, and become very codependent upon their favors.

This is especially true for women as well, who have an even more difficult time trying to gain the necessary financial independence, so vital to their personal freedom as well. Mafia is the direct result of ignorance, villainous behaviors and criminal inclination.

I strongly feel that my situation and condition in Italy could have been very different if I had not had to deal with such an ignorant socio-economical background. This is true for both my sexual and financial sphere. However, I cannot wait for Italians to grow up.

The time I was granted on Earth is not endless, and I surely cannot wait for things to change in order to improve my life conditions. I leave it up to them to deal with their crap. I just have got to figure out the best possible strategy for my own benefit.

I have also decided to stop writing in Italian, as I feel that is just a waste of time and resources on my end. Italians at large are just one big ghetto family, and I really have no intension to keep trying to educate them. I think I have already done more than enough.

After all, I have many times said that philosophy is just a philanthropy's tool in order not to lose track of man's walk in his earthly space-time dimension. If one understands philanthropy, he or she cannot but understand the culture one is born in is irrelevant.

On the same line of thought, often I think about my attraction for American women as an inevitable consequence based upon historical events. For instance, my father always telling me that we originally came from Germany is not coincidence either.

In fact, in my mind is pretty obvious that being America nothing more but the Latin feminine word for Amerigo Vespucci's first name, and being him an Italian man, I couldn't but love American women, especially blonds, like most Germans.

Furthermore, not only Jesus Christ is often depicted blond in art, but the Bible itself describes the Nazarites just like that, blond with blue eyes, pale complexion and blushing. And it is not by chance the turmoil of WWII originated in Germany either.

It is not by chance I have often referred to the original sin and the snake bearing clear sexual meanings as well either, particularly when in comes down to black-white intermixing, therefore agreeing with Muhammad Ali, those should not be recommended.

It is also obvious that because of the very nature of the issues I address in my writings, many may wonder what my final aim is, or what I am trying to achieve with my researches and speculations. However, all I am trying to do is getting to know myself.

In fact, I strongly believe that in order not to cause any harm onto others, one must really and foremost know himself and herself deeply and thoroughly. That is also why I do not shine away from openly addressing sex and eroticism in my writings.

By now, my metric should have given a pretty clear idea of its redundant themes and topics. In a way, I have tried to put in writing the biological, natural cycles of my own mind, as I live and perceive them throughout my day by day human experience.

I don't even think it's a coincidence that blonds and redheads are on the edge of extinction either. Perhaps my own writings are an attempt to let my own personality and psyche come loose, as in an attempt to have others analyze, consider and evaluate it.

In fact, should blonds go extinct, I might as well go with them. By that I don't mean giving up my life, but simply accepting the fact that beings like me and those pretty blonds are just going to be the next dinosaurs on Earth one very distant day.

That is also the reason why, in my opinion, many blonds breed with black people. In a way they are just putting up with the idea there might be no future for them on Earth, so they might as well resign, go black, and never having to coming back white again.

At least they have a pussy, which is much more valuable than a dick like the one I have. I mean, they can give it away much easier than I'll ever be able to. I can try putting my dick on sale and nobody will want to have it; just not the case for pussy.

In a way, all I am trying to do here is to ask questions, just like the Socratic Method, and nothing more. I do not even pretend having all answers to such questions, but at least I have the proof I asked them myself and to others, in an attempt to find answers.

The goal here is to get the brain thinking, stimulating neurons to do their job, and hoping to get and extra bonus with such elaborate questioning such as living an overall longer and healthier life, full of pussy, boobs, kisses and breath taking undies and lingerie.

As all things in life, the problem is not building, but maintaining. It's just like to Romans who aimed at defeating all deserts by building their aqueducts and bringing water in the most arid regions. My writings are like water, wishing to irrigate dry souls.

One person alone may be able to build several aqueducts or to write a few books, however he or she is destined to fail if nobody will pick up the task of contributing to the overall effort, ensuring the necessary maintenance is provided afterwards, like in politics.

Perhaps, this is just what I am seeking in life. Like Paulo Coelho, whose writings have also impacted the global economical stage; I put no limits to my thought as segregation is counterproductive for every human being, independently of his or her nationality.

After all, I see many similarities with Pablo Neruda's life as well. Despite I was never really sent on exile, I feel like my life has been just like that; always in constant exile. At least he had some female company while living in Italy, on the island of Capri.

Poets' involvement in the political events that characterize their times is absolutely normal and spontaneous in my opinion. In fact, a poet's ultimate goal is to educate humanity in order to facilitate its progress; unless he or she is more inclined toward the dark side, of course.

In such case, when poets decant too much melancholy, negativity and pessimism in their writings, they end up fomenting depression rather than optimism and positive emotions. The same is for those poets who instigate the use of drugs and hallucinogenic to evade reality.

Given that the gift of poetry is granted to humans with great responsibility, it is always up to the individual to apply his or her free will in all decisions they are faced to make. In a way, one could say that being a poet is like being a category at risk for the public order.

Now that I know that, and that I wrote it, I have no more excused ignoring the possible impact my writing could have on the future society as much as the one I live in right now. Poets are visionaries, yet not divine beings, therefore they must be very prudent.

So, can this new era or New World Order be a positive and good thing for humanity, rather than a return to old imperialist ideals and dreams? I certainty believe so. Ignoring the fact this change is inevitable and trying to contrast it is just insane.

One can only try to accept the changes ahead and take proper actions to ensure such changes will be for the good of humanity, and not aimed to project it back to darkness and medieval way of living. Therefore, everyone can contribute to its success.

This new world scenario still has many challenges ahead to face. At first, I was very skeptic too, while learning the issues for the first time. Yet, after having studied and learned more deeply about it, I came to realize that the New World Order is inevitable.

Italians have the right to their opinion and say on the issue as well. However, they must also understand they are a minority on this planet, and that the democratic process of the world, taking place at the United Nations, is not something they can ignore.

We owe it to future generations more than ourselves. If I enjoyed the fruits of post WWII progress and prosperity, which were only possible because of peace, the same I must grant to future generations. Only in this optic the world can find a new balance.

We owe it to future generations more than ourselves. If I enjoyed the fruits of post WWII progress and prosperity, which were only possible because of peace, the same I must grant to future generations. Only in this optic the world can find a new balance.

I guess I also owed it to my second cousin, the Italian airman Francesco Paga, who lost his life cannibalized in Congo, in the Kindu Massacre, while serving for the United Nations. May his sacrifice, as many others' more, not pass onto history as in vain.

So far, my life has been filled with way too much tragedy, to the point should it ever be the theme of a drama, I'd feel very disappointed it being too tragic, rather than more of a comedy drama as well. I feel I handle my personal tragedies pretty well.

Actually, it is only because o my positive and comic attitude I can offset the tragic influences coming from all around me at this point in time. A drama itself is a staged act, therefore my life a drama, and I am the main character of my screenplay.

I freely choose not to take part to a tragic drama, but rather join a comedy instead. A part from the fact the public mass does not even realize a drama is not a tragedy itself, just like real life is not meant to be that either. It's up to us choosing what to make of it.

The New World Order may seem a tragedy to many, yet it is more of a comedy instead, meaning that its purpose is to infuse joyfulness, not pity and guiltiness. The New World Order can be a positive vibe so to speak, rather than a negative one.

I also must honestly and without arrogance say to have contributed to shining some light on some legal loopholes within the NATO block, therefore both in the U.S. and Europe. One was filled by the European Parliament, after I reported Mario Draghi for usury.

Perhaps it was just this inclination of mine toward justice and the implementation of the law that got me in so much trouble with criminals or immoral villains in general. I could just never stand illegal grounds or even unregulated matters and situations.

I always liked living knowing my limits, especially my legal ones. Just as a computing machine, I would get confused and impatient when facing a situation without a clear legal regulation telling me how to behave. Computation without inputs is not possible.

In a way, the New World Order cannot take into account the information technology age as a true and evolving fact and phenomena. Information technology, machines and binary codes have strongly influenced the way I think for example.

I am not saying I no longer feel human, but a machine instead. I have said that for my nationality, as I feel American, no longer Italian. However, that is not the case for my binary thinking. Nevertheless, I constantly confront my mind with machines.

I do believe, even in this fast evolving technology age, survival is still a matter of mind over machine, and never the contrary. People who are not so technologically advanced may perceive me just as cold machine or a robot, rather than a human being with feelings.

In Iowa, I can say being responsible for having created a precedent in Common law, due to my action of flashing my dick at the FBI in Davenport, in my home. Well, I was acquitted innocent as I did not have an erection, therefore without any sexual connotations.

This is just another example of what the New World Order really is about. It is about ensuring the legal system is put in place to serve citizens, rather than to enslave them. I have always trusted the law and courts, and used it to defend myself and my rights.

Thinking the world could go back to barbarism and self defense is not exactly what our predecessors would have wished for us. Now, I am not saying I am in favor of one global centralized government; however I do support an active round table at the United Nations.

I actually feel I have been in jail since I moved back to Italy. And that's another reason why I do not ever want to represent Italians on this planet. Actually, so far, in my life, I have been able to collect the hate of both Americans and Italians toward me.

That's why I feel nobody loves me. Americans have investigated and put me in jail for one night. Italians are so ignorant that living among them is just like living in jail as well. I have no luck with Italian women, and can't get an American one either.

I hate my life right now. How the hell did I get myself into so much trouble I don't even know. Perhaps it was just my curiosity to get me where I am right now. Yet, I can't but say that could I go back, I would do it again, just the way I did. Or, may be, not quite.

What is even funnier is that I have always preferred knowledge over pussy, and that might be the cause of all my problems too. I mean, I lost my virginity when I was twenty two, and thought to be tremendously in love with the right person, who was just like me.

Then I ended up divorcing, meeting a bunch more of other neurotic and lunatic girlfriends. Had I thought about fucking sooner, would it have been better for me? I guess I'll never find the answer to that one, as I cannot change my past and my story either.

The only thing that could save me, other than getting a job on a cruise ship, would be winning a Nobel in literature. And I am not saying it for the glory as much as for the prize itself, which would at least allow me to go on vacation abroad, and hopefully get laid.

I mean, the people in Venafro are so ignorant they didn't even realize they had Pontius Pilate's home right there in front of them. I had to come all the way from the States to tell them just that, and they became even angrier at me saying I was stupid.

Life is really strange, I can assure you that. I even sent the story to UNESCO in Paris, in order to candidate Venafro to World Heritage Site. I mean, I have tried it all to make some bucks, but it's just true when they say art doesn't grant you a penny.

At least I was hoping art would get me laid, but in my case, not even that. I can't but start laughing at myself for the situation I am in right now. Instead of watching television to entertain myself, I might as well make a comedy out of my own life.

I have often thought about stop writing, many many times. Perhaps time has come to really make a final decision in that direction. It would probably be better for me if I planned on finishing this book and stop writing afterwards, to start focusing on an income.

I can't go on like this for ever in life. I am getting older, and despite the world seems going down the drain, I am smart enough to understand the current events are not necessarily going to affect me directly, if I am well prepared to face the challenges ahead.

Once again, I have tried to teach others more than I have spent time thinking about myself, and now I have realized I can no longer continue down this road. Things are just not happening the way I'd like. What else can I do? Better being honest to one's self.

At least I'll always be able to say I tried them all in order to achieve my goals and my dreams. It's just that they do not always come true, and one must understand that's just the way it is, and it should have been known before embarking in such adventure.

Therefore I have no regrets what's so ever. Following my dreams has been fun so far, and very rewarding, even if only humanly, and not financially. I can say to have had a pretty healthy life so far, in terms of physical and emotional health, despite my complaints.

Plus, one can never know for sure. I mean, what I have created is going to stay for ever, even after the end of my journey. I am sure once I'll be very old, looking back at all my stories, I am going to be very pleased with myself for all I have done.

On top of it all, since the patron saint of Venafro is St. Nicander, many here bear that name. However, because local people don't even speak proper Italian, but a dialect instead, when they shorten it by saying St. Nica', I always understand St. Nigga.

Even the roosters here in Venafro seem to be singing, "Saint Nigga!" instead of the American "cock-a-doodle" or call of a cockerel. I think animals are influenced by their surroundings as much as humans are, and tone to local dialects as well.

I should probably ask a rooster how the hell I can get laid over here in Venafro, as I can't even find one single chick willing to let me play the cock of the walk. And I am not even asking to have my own henhouse, but just a little fun along the way.

I have even thought about freeing up a few quails and pheasants on Mount Holy Cross, but I don't have the money to buy them in the first place. I guess only roosters can figure out how to manage a henhouse without cash, as for me seems pretty impossible.

After all, how could I blame women for enjoying and desiring the good life? Not that life is all about money, but is surely helps conducting a better existence. In a way, having a vagina is already a certain advantage, due to its motivating power.

However, the idea that pussy is the driving force behind all existence is pretty disparaging for a man, despite that's just the simplest of all truths. I guess, that's where the fear of women being also in control of money comes from, in the Arab world.

I wish I could offer myself as slave to a woman; at least that would end my agony. After almost five years of agony, I have realized I cannot live without pussy. But, because women own pussy, it does not come free. Like it or not, you can't get pussy without woman.

Now, some women may give it away for money, and that's just fine, despite that is illegal in many places; just not in Las Vegas or Amsterdam. Other women may only want their pussy scratched inside once in a while; despite they may not say it that way.

Then, there are those women who are gonna give their pussy unless you get the entire package with it, and not just for one ride. Now, they wish men were able to understand the kind of women they were just by looking at them; but I am just not that good.

Sometimes I wish both men and women were a bit more mature and honest to one another, especially expressing their needs, desires and fantasies. Prejudice on the topic is the source of secrecy, especially when it comes down to money and finance.

In fact, money can assure a certain level of privacy, therefore security for both men and women. So, once again, if one cannot change human psychology, there is nothing left to do than trying to change the root cause of his poverty, such as in my case.

In a way, so far in my life, I have done everything possible to address the root causes of my uncertain monetary and financial conditions, mostly linked to macro economical factors, which got me in trouble because they are of national security relevance.

I mean, I can honestly say that pussy is the only sole accountable for my disastrous life! Had I not desired pussy so much, perhaps I wouldn't have gotten myself in all the troubles I did. And thank God I even started late with pussy in my life, at twenty two!

Though, I really cannot prove my curiosity was unconsciously driven and motivated by the desire and dripping for pussy. Therefore I don't really have a case there. I am afraid dealing with pussy is just like with money. If you don't have it, you're fucked.

Once again, I cannot but hope for Hillary Clinton to become the first female U.S. President, just because that way, women may become more generous, even with the losers like me. That is the best New World Order I can imagine; the one where I can get laid.

In a way, a female President would be just the perfect beginning of a New World Order, fully invested with symbolism of true, permanent and positive shift in human consciousness, and a new revolutionary approach to sexuality, psychology and sociology.

I can honestly and sincerely say that, if white women breed with blacks rather than me, that's probably because the white man has a share of responsibility in this behavior. That being the white man has not be treating properly and accordingly his life companions.

I have even been considering that perhaps my bad luck with women, lately, is due to lack of aphrodisiac foods intake. I wonder if a new, better and more in depth look at the Codex Alimentarius may actually reveal some clues on how to improve performance.

Actually, despite I love the Mediterranean diet, as recognized by UNESCO, I happen to be a bit bored by the Italian cuisine alone. I miss the diversity of foods and cuisines I was used to in the States. In fact, I profess a Mediterranean cuisine open to internationalism.

Of course, being able to enjoy food with the other sex is also vital for the relationship itself, and not only for good sex. It is hard enjoy a balanced partition of Mediterranean diet, as core cuisine, with other culinary traditions to fulfill and complement it daily.

That's hard not because of its practicability, but due to one's tastes and preference more than the difficulty of following such a diet itself. It takes pretty open minded women to seat at my table on a daily base, and sharing and enjoying the pleasure of good meals.

Once again, this kind of female, happy meals partner has greater possibilities to be found in America rather than Italy. Italian women are still attached to their traditional cuisine, despite the changes seen with the opening of new ethnical restaurants.

I only hope not to sound too picky in terms of all the qualities I look for and seek in a woman. I mean, I am not looking for all that at once just to get laid. However, I am convinced that the quality of good sex is strictly connected to a couple's overall compatibility.

It's just mathematical; the more compatible a couple is the better sex they have. Now, what compatible really means is a complete different story, and I am afraid to be not the best person to write on the matter, especially by judging my bed accomplishments.

Talking about the Codex Alimentarius, in the past I had problems with my girlfriends because of my reluctance using food coloring and additives in general. However, the point they never understood is that I don't oppose them, just the amounts in the daily diet.

For instance, I have obviously used GMOs while living the United States, and been always very cautious about them. Nevertheless, now that I see failure to feed the entire world's population means starvation, and with it comes war, I came to accept them.

I guess many women may even have looked at me as some kind of primitive, just because of my consciousness in approaching new things, especially when it came down to their direct impact on my body. Well, I guess smoking marijuana was contradicting.

I figured, there is no way the WHO and FAO could really put their efforts together in order to develop and try to enforce the Codex Alimentarius with the only purpose of depopulate this planet. That may even be a possibility, just not the best solution for any of us.

Now, these are the moles of shit I constantly run in my mind, and I am not sure any women may actually want to be next to such a nerd or even a dork like me. However, I am being just sarcastic, as I don't really have issues related to self-esteem, or just not yet.

And, as if my troubles weren't enough yet, I'm afraid I'll have to give up smoking too. I pretty much done with the school year, and I am not going to have an income here shortly. I am not going to be able to keep buying my Natural American Spirit tobacco any more.

That was my only vice keeping me company for about two years now, since I started smoking out of loneliness. Well, I still have about six months worth of Playboy's issues, as for my masturbation needs, but I wish I had a little ganja to smoke too.

My relation with marijuana has also always been very peculiar too. I must honestly admit to have always enjoyed it, despite it was and still is illegal in many nations within the NATO block. However, that is the only case I have broken the law in my lifetime.

I understand that drugs are a very bad business to get involved with, especially because it provides finances to the black market, which in return uses these illicit funds often to finance actions of terrorism or aimed at destabilize security within the NATO block.

So, I have been responsible for that in my life, several times; despite I have always confessed my belief for decriminalizing the use of cannabis so that I could have bought it paying taxes too, and making sure none of my money ended up in the hands of terrorists.

However, it's Christ commanding me to obey the Law. Had it not been for Him, the whole Army as we know it today wouldn't even exist, as soldiers obey orders, and we would have succumbed to crazy fanatics like Hitler and many others before and after him.

What I mean by that is, despite the fact I have never practiced my religion in an orthodox way, Christ taught me that by willingly choosing the die accordingly to the sentence He was granted. Not even He opposed the law of men, despite being God.

Actually, my peculiar spirituality also created many frictions with women in the past. They thought because I didn't feel like going to church was a sign of my lack of faith. Nothing could have been farther from truth; despite I never talked of Jesus as my Lord.

I always lived faith as an intimate time of reconnection with the source and rejuvenation. In a way I always felt I had overcome many of the issues addressed by religious teachings, which many still struggle with, and that's not wanting to be arrogant.

Perhaps, it's just that I am so bored right now; I have nothing else to do than letting my mind loose and writing my thoughts as fast as they reach my consciousness from who knows where. In a way, I always said finding writing very therapeutic too.

People may not realize it by seeing me; however I do carry lots of overweight baggage with me. My experiences have made me who I am right now, and that's something I cannot regret, or such feeling will make my life unlivable and unbearable.

Only later in life I understood I had to take a clear stand on faith and religion. In fact, for too long I thought, just as the law says, it did not matter. However, in real life I came to realize that people still judge one's religion as much as sexual orientation.

In a way, that's just like my vice, which makes me break the law at times to smoke some pot. I guess others would rather force the law the same way to understand what your stand is on religion or sexual orientation. Therefore, I cannot complain about it too much.

Perhaps, it's just that Italians are too apathetic, therefore don't mind their business, while I am too passionate about life, and that's why they stalk me instead. Perhaps that was just the same while I was living the United States as well; I don't know for sure.

Perhaps the problem is not just apathy, and as I have already said before, it is a real criminal issue linked to envy for what I have achieved so far in artistic and business matters. However, I don't even have money to buy myself tobacco anymore.

Like Ezra Pound, and many other poets, I have always been very passionate about politics too. However, unlike Pound, I have never crossed the border and passed from writing to acting, if not permitted, to disrupt any Governmental activity or organization.

For such a reason I do not feel I have ever committed any crime toward any institution within the NATO block, other than always fully used my rights, and participated to public life accordingly, also by openly expressing my thoughts and my comments.

In a way, I feel the NATO block has only benefited by my political participation, also when it was in the form of strong criticism toward the policies which were being implemented time to time. I don't regret that kind of activism as it is the source of my passion.

Had I not been so passionate about my political participation I would have never been able to transfer such passion into my lines. Nevertheless, I always felt the importance of respecting the law and trying to do my best to always behave within those limits.

All of that may also have scared women, or it's just that I never really surrounded myself with the right type of woman who could have stood by my side firmly. So, I payed the price for trying to live my love life while cultivating all my interests at the same time.

Right now I feel just like St. Augustine writing his confessions, and despite it hurts, as usual when I open my heart and write my feelings, I know that tomorrow I'll be very glad having it done today. Once one puts something in writing, it becomes obsolete.

Thank God I don't have to worry abut food and shelter, despite I pay a very high price for it. In fact, living home with my parents is driving me insane, because I can't really stand my mother, especially when I get up and see her first thing in the morning.

What I just said is blasphemy to Italians, who are well known for loving their mothers more than their wives. I hope that was not how my ex-wife felt about my mother, contributing to the end of our marriage, as she may have influenced all my relationships.

I mean, I ended up referring to her as "mama nigga," especially because the people here in Venafro live just like in the ghettos, and the patron saint is St. Nigga, according to what they call St. Nicander. Now, that doesn't help picking up chicks in Italy either.

She is constantly spying me, making noises right above my room. She is constantly trying to listen to any single sound I make in the room downstairs, and even more disgusting, she is always sniffing when I walk by, as if she were a fucking dog. It's senile dementia.

So, because the school year is about finished and I have just a few lesson left before the summer break, I have decided to write a note to one of my colleagues. Her name is Nina, and she's from Brussels. She a very pretty, tiny brunette with dark skin.

Now, it's not that I expect she is going to get laid with me after reading my post-it, nevertheless a bit of romance in life is absolutely necessary. So, I wrote her, "Nina, you're so petite, you stimulate my appetite." I hope she is going to get the rhyme.

Actually, just a few evenings ago we had a pizza party with the school, and I told her, "Voulez vous coucher avec moi ce soir?" That being French for, "will you sleep with me tonight?" She obviously speaks French as well being from Belgium.

However, I am afraid she didn't understand I was being serious. Oh well; I guess having Italian parents makes her culturally Italian as well, not like me. I guess Italian women do not like such sharpness and direct language or proposals, but it's my style.

The fact I don't like hiding who I really am also implies I respect other people's way of life and freedom of expression, including their right not to express what their intentions or feelings really are. It's just that she was so hot in her light, red summer dress!

After all, impressionism started right in France, in Paris exactly. Painters like Monet, Sisley, Renoir, Pissarro, Morisot, Cassatt, Degas, Manet, Guillaumin, Caillebotte and Bazille have laid the foundations to imagism in poetry in the 19th century.

Impressionists aimed at transferring a clear impression in their paintings, focusing on accurate depiction of light in its changing qualities. Not by chance, in the 20th century, Ezra Pound declares imagism isolates objects through the use of "luminous details."

What impressionists and imagists try to do is transferring onto others a whole set of emotions though one single scene. It is just like trying to decipher all information contained within a single photon which only allows to be perceived through a single image.

Michael Davidson kind of saw this right by saying that Pound's ideogrammic method of juxtaposing concrete instances to express an abstraction is similar to cubism's manner of synthesizing multiple perspectives into a single image[1].

---

1 Davidson, Michael (1997). Ghostlier demarcations: modern poetry and the material word. University of California Press, pp. 11–13. ISBN 0-520-20739-4

However, photons do not alter the shape of an object in order to deliver their messages, yet they portray the object just as it is and how, perhaps, it was meant to be; that's why imagism in closer and more strictly related to impressionism rather than cubism.

It was inevitable that painting first started to express such emotions through the mostly common understood form of communicative art, i.e. visual communication such as painting. This gave poetry the opportunity to refine the style into the written form of imagism.

In fact, while impressionists tried to communicate through very precise images, the ultimate goal was that of touching or reaching another person's soul at an emotional level. Ezra Pound aimed at the very same result, through the trickier art of using words.

However, this overall modern artistic tendency beginning with impressionism and soon after acquired by imagists, is trying to prepare the ground for another kind of human communication, but always through the use of images carrying emotions.

If emotions where at first transferred with an image through a painting, then these images where just simply described through words, now there would be no need for any kind of medium at all. Images can be transferred telepathically from one brain to another.

With images telepathically transferred from one being to another, a new form of visual and conceptual communication would arise. Telepathy will be able to deliver visual, conceptual emotions more efficiently across human's integument membranes.

In a way, I can say to have noticed this tendency in contemporary painting as well, by observing some of the works of a friend, the American painter Tess Logan, from Portland, whom I have also dated once. She studied at Central Saint Martins, in London.

Her abstracts where literally infused with earthly aromas as well, just as an attempt, in my opinion, to link such surreal visions to reality itself. In a way, that's exactly what telepathy is trying to accomplish, by bridging the gap between ideas and reality.

I have also noticed the same attempts in paintings in Italy as well, through the works of an Italian painter by the name of Giuseppe Attanasio, whom I have known since in my childhood, while growing up in Cicciano. He is also a meticulous light observer.

Not only that, but once again I have noticed just that in the works of another abstract American painter, the brother of an ex-girlfriend of mine, whom I dated in Davenport. His name is Kevin Jr. Lonergan, and his brushing technique was quite charming.

Funny enough, I think Kevin studied at the Art Institute of Chicago, and his sister Kear, whom I dated, was a hairdresser, who brushed my hair several times, and gave me several hair cuts while I was living in Davenport. But that story didn't end well either.

I must also confess being greatly impressed by contemporary Russian abstract art, including the philologist Marina Orlova. Russian's abstract space scene paintings are also underlying how mankind is already projecting itself out of the usual dimensions.

As one can see, the stage is set for the New World Order to finally take place and replace the old living habits. Ignoring not only what politicians are doing, but what art is telling us as well is suicide, just like complaining but making always the same mistakes.

In a way, the same way imagism was a consequence of impressionism, abstract art is a consequence of imagism. This is how humanity goes up and down the ladder of evolution and progress. Artists are therefore visionaries, able to anticipate times.

One can even look at China to see a concrete example of how all around the globe there are clear signs shining light onto the darkness of human condition, and perhaps loneliness in the universe, despite all its challenges that Country is still facing.

Looking at the progress China has made so far makes me feel even more ashamed of being born in Italy, due its still so primitive inhabitants. No wonder I cannot relate to Italian people, starting from my own family of origin and the land I grew up.

The problem is that I understand Italy will eventually join the ride, just like during World War II. However, I cannot waste my lifetime babysitting them or waiting for them to live up to the challenges of the 21st century. I have the right to live my own life.

I surely cannot tell for sure if I'll spend the rest of my life here in Italy; however, I surely have the right to live here taking care of my own interests independently of what Italians think, as long as I live within the limits granted and imposed by the law.

In a way, my writings reflect just that, which is the hardship and reluctance of Italian culture to accept change, despite that is not impossible to accomplish. If I have made it, Italians at large can too. However, in the process, I have also rejected my Italian origin.

I guess, it's really only up to them to decide how to proceed in this constantly changing and evolving globalization scenario, without loosing their identity. Surely, I would recommend young Italians to explore Italian poetry just as I did with English.

I am actually curious to see what Italian poets may look like in the future, as I consider myself an American poet, not Italian. I am sure Italy will surprise me in the future, and I look forward to see what the italic ingenuity will be capable of achieving.

Just as Winston Churchill noticed about Italians and their peculiar ability to flip side accordingly during WWII, so I did. At first they were all about Mussolini, and then they ended up hanging him. At least, I only happened to learn English and boycott Italian.

Had Italians created better opportunities for me and the rest of my generation, perhaps this would have never happened, and I would have never boycotted Italian. However, things went differently in my case, and I can only hope it never happens again in the future.

Plus, such things are pretty normal too, and they are permitted and allowed by the law. I am surely not the first or the last one who actually ends up living in a different part of the planet he or she was originally from. But I am a poet, so I wrote about it.

Without kidding, my life has been just like Dante's spiral journey from hell to heaven so far. The only problem is that I haven't reached heaven yet. I don't even think that's a coincidence his journey focused around a female figure as well, Beatrice.

You see, even Dante Alighieri couldn't help but feeling the divine, driving force of a pussy behind all his writing. Once can pretend that's just not the case, however I can ensure everyone that had it not been for pussy, I would have never started writing.

As a matter of fact, it was just Kear, the ex-girlfriend of mine, and abstract American painter Kevin Lonergan's sister, who got me into writing. I guess it was because of her Irish pride, free and challenging behavior I felt had to nail her down somehow.

It was right after we broke up I started writing my first book, and ever since I haven't been able to stop writing. In a way I feel I loved her as much as all my poetry altogether and I started writing just to make her feel all my love. I can't regret that either.

At times I have even considered trying to get back together; I even wrote her that the only thing I regretted about our relationship was not having had a child with her. However, I am not sure that getting back with an ex partner is a good idea in general.

As a matter of fact, once Kear was right here in Venafro too, as she came with me to Italy for Christmas one year, visiting my parents. Luckily enough, I didn't know what Venafro was really like back then, and didn't even know about Pontius Pilate's villa either.

It doesn't look like even Playboy has ever taken a clear, net stand on the issue of getting back together with an ex love partner. I mean, I don't know for experience, but have read both positive and negative comments and articles on the topic, which is pretty hot.

In a way I feel I wouldn't even be considering the issue if I didn't have to. If I had a new girlfriend at the moment I wouldn't even think about my exes for sure. Despite the fact this one time I was with Kear, she caught me still taking a look at my ex wife's videos.

As a matter of fact, Kear was my ex wife's friend, before becoming my new girlfriend. Actually, that's another hot topic right there. Would you consider dating one or more of your ex's friends acceptable and even auspicial, or to be completely avoided?

To be, or not to be? That is the question according to Shakespeare. Personally, I'd rather be than not, but that's just my opinion. Therefore, rather than spending the rest of my life alone, I'll prefer getting back with my exes, or even any friends of any my exes.

But, given that, granted the opportunity, I'll always have a fresh new beginning with a new girlfriend, or even more than one, rather than getting back into a dysfunctional relationship. In love, as much as in business, it's all about risk and asset management.

And that's pretty much why I am broke and penniless. I guess my ex-girlfriend Kear just influenced me way too much with that Irish nonsense limerick style. Taken in very small doses, it can be even fun. However, an overdose of limerick nonsense is lethal!

Another issue I had, always with Italian-Americans even in the States always concerns women. I dated this chick from Des Moines named Kristina, and eventually she ended up having a kid and getting involved with an older mobster from Chicago.

I mean, Italians have always and only been a source of troubles in my life, and never brought anything good to actually improve my living conditions, both financially and emotionally. The fact I can no longer stand Italians has precise psychological reasons.

The only happy memories I have with an ex-girlfriend are the moments spent with a ballerina of the Ballet Quad Cities, Margaret Huling. We were both just coming out of a relationship, and honestly got in a temporary companionship without commitment.

We were basically friends with benefits so to speak. We had very good sex, and romantic dinners as well. One night, I even ended up meeting her boss, a choreographer who had actually worked years before in Italy, at the Real Teatro di San Carlo in Naples.

I have always lived without real physical and cultural borders within the NATO block, and honestly, I really think everyone should be able to have such a vast selection of possibilities. I hope the New World Order will ensure and promote just that.

By the way, I left the post-it onto Nina's desk today, at school. She was not there though, so I am not sure what she will think when reads it. I wish I was able to see her face while reading it, rather than asking if she read it. Oh well, things like that happen.

I think the New World Order is inevitable simple because the freedom I have experienced in my life is at risk. As a matter of fact, it's the overall Western civilization philosophy and way of living to be at stake here. Too many hate the Western life.

At first I have looked at the anti New World Order supporters as rightly protesting against another upcoming totalitarian attempt. However, when I experienced first hand what their alternative was, I realized they were once against just offering communism.

Communism had never really been an alternative to the New World Order in my mind, and it would be a much more horrible condition for humanity than a society based upon the most simple prevention and respect of laws and order in the best public interest.

Everything I was able to experience in my life would have never been possible under a communist regime. Furthermore, communism nowadays is nothing more than an excuse for terrorists to influence Western youth in order to join their cause.

I surely don't believe communism will get me laid more, or will ensure me a more promiscuous and satisfying sexual life. Communists are as close minded as Islamic integralists and terrorists can be. History speaks by itself, and I didn't write it.

Actually, communism would only be the perfect substratum for terrorism, including mafia, to preserve their illicit wealth and activities. That's why I strongly disagree and dislike the political ideologies of Italian communist writer Antonio Gramsci.

As a matter of fact, I owe NATO the freedom I have experienced and am most grateful to its work since it was created after World War II, with the specific mission to contrast and prevent the communist threat from sinking Europe and the States once again.

I am a little disappointed that mobsters, terrorists, gangsters and drug dealers get all the pussy while I starve. And, I surely don't want any pussy they passed before me. I mean, would you rather wear new shoes or used ones? I like brand new shoes.

I hope I'll make a good parody of what I don't like about the Old World Order in order to make sure the New World Order won't be just like the old one, bland, no spice at all and scarce in terms of all kinds of natural resources, especially money and pussy.

Were I asked to choose just one thing to bring with me into the New World Order, I'd have a very hard time. For instance, with money, the old fashion way, you can get all the pussy you want. But, if you have lots of pussy, what do you need money for?

In a way, I also owed this book to Virgil, who coined the phrase Novus Order Seclorum, and whose tomb is in Naples, just a few hours away from Venafro, not too far from the U.S Consulate either. After all, the West is tightly linked to ancient Rome.

Now, not that I want to sound too arrogant, but Virgil was a poet as well, therefore I am honored mentioning him in my own memories as the father of the New World Order. Yet, by saying that, I am not wishing to resuscitate Caesar or the Roman Empire.

Actually, I truly hope the New World Order will not make the same mistakes of ancient Rome. At least, we have a rotten model to look at and confront our accomplishments with. Nevertheless, times have changed, and Jesus was born soon after Virgil.

Anyhow, having visited Pompeii many times, I know for a fact that brothels were pretty common back then, and ancient Romans have to enjoy their sexuality very much. With that, I wouldn't want to go from total abstinence all the way to sexual addiction either.

Therefore, I hope for a more sexually opened and mature New World Order, where a certain attention to sexually transmitted diseases would still overcome the animal instinct of just fucking around. Of course, there should also be room for virginity as well.

Not all human beings are born equal. We are all equal by law, yet not biologically. Some are straight and others are gay; as much as some are monogamists or polygamists, which happen to be illegal, for God sake. But, some decide to be virgin till marriage.

I don't see anything wrong with one living up to his or her sexual desires, as long as those do not offend anyone else. And I am not saying that in a moral sense only, but physically or legally if you like. Humanity has been slave to sexuality for too long now.

Bottom line, let's just hope I'm gonna get some pussy with this New World Order. That's all I ask after years of involuntary abstinence. I really need to get laid, and funny enough, the only time I need it the most, nobody tells me that's just what I need.

I am just a loser. I don't even seem to inspire any pity at all. I mean, if nuns were really so willing to help others; well, I am not saying they should let me fuck with them, but at least they could hook me up with a hooker in exchange for some English lessons.

My mind must be really perverted. I was trying to explain a student from Venafro the difference between a metaphor and a simile in literature. I couldn't think about any better examples for such figure of speech than nigga and zenga; latter short for zengar.

Now, in a metaphor, a poet implies that nigga and zenga, pronounced zoo, egg and so forth, are the same thing, therefore there can be no direct reference to either blacks or gypsies. A simile implies that black people are like gypsies, but not the same.

I don't understand why I can't come out with better example to explain certain things to the public. Perhaps it's just because I was traumatized behind recovery when my father took me to visit the tomb of our cannibalized cousin in Pisa, when I was seven.

Perhaps that's also the reason why I cannot get laid. I am way too stressed by seeing an increase of black people around me and so many blonds breeding with them. I mean, I must be unconsciously terrorized of ending up just like my second cousin, cannibalized.

I hope the New World Order is going to protect me from being cannibalized. But more than anything else, I wish for the New World Order to get me laid by the end of the year. Actually, I don't even care about being cannibalized, as long as I can get laid first.

I don't know what will happen by the time I finish writing this book. Will have I gotten laid, or won't have I? This is the question. As usual, my answer is always that I'd rather get laid than lying alone in bed. Sexual abstinence is very unhealthy for my psyche.

I cannot help but laugh at the assonances of the Neapolitan language, mostly due to Italy's long history of contrast with Saracen and Arab culture in general. In fact, five words seem to be reoccurring all the time, "allah, nigga, zenga, villa, and babba."

Now, the first three words are pretty self-explanatory to any English speaker. Villa however is not referring to a house, but a villain instead. Whereas, babba is the name of Naples' most popular dessert, soft and juicy just like a fine cut prime pussy.

Had I not learned English, I would have never been able to look at Italian culture as an outsider, therefore catching up on those assonances and cultural references to Italy's thousand years long history. But this might also be the root cause of my cultural shock.

I am afraid not even Virgil may believe how elegant and eloquent his old Latin language has become over the course of history. Nevertheless, such specific, ethnical oriented philology cannot be but a niche in linguistics; difficult for anthropologists as well.

I actually wouldn't mind banging Russian philologist Marina Orlova either, despite I am afraid Neapolitan philology will drive her crazy too. Just as British singer Sting felt as an alien in New York, I feel an alien in Italy too, despite I was born in Turin.

I guess Muslims would like me to convert to Islam, promising me a whole harem, if I only joined their belief or creed. That would be actually pretty appealing, if only I didn't have to become circumcised. In that case, I'd rather convert to Judaism.

Actually, being Christian of Jewish ancestry made me reflect a lot on circumcision as well. I am not circumcised; despite at the age of sixteen I got my frenulum removed with a frenectomy. I am very happy about that, as I am marked, but still have my prepuce.

I feel like I would recommend the same to my own children, especially in order to remember we were of Jewish ancestry, yet not following the Jewish religion, but Christians instead. Also, the age of sixteen is a good time to have a frenectomy in my opinion.

However, quite honestly, circumcision, frenectomy or none of them does me no good if I can't even get laid in the first place. I am afraid all my sexual torments are tightly linked to summertime heat, and a subsequent uncontrollable testosterone level.

As a matter of fact, in the New World Order fathers have a new role in the sexual education of their children, especially their daughters. It is up to them teaching their daughters everything abut penis, without delegating this sensitive task to the mothers.

As far as fathers teaching their sons about vaginas; well, that's still up to Playboy, for God sake! It's about time for men to contribute actively to the sexual education of their children, helping their spouses as a true New World Order gentleman would do.

The other thing I am really craving and can't get in Italy, other than pussy of course, is bison or buffalo meat. Juicy buffalo hamburgers are just like a nicely shaved juicy pussy. And, when cooked rare or medium rare, even the pink color is the same.

I hope for the New World Order to be more ecologically and environmentally concerned. If bison's go extinct, it would be just like blonds going extinct. I'll have absolutely no motivation or interests left in a world without buffalos and blond haired pussies.

Another bizarre thing I have noticed over here is the false believes still so popular among the average people. For instance, Italians, just like Arabs, still believe that when a child is conceived, paternity is influenced by the penetration of previous partners.

Also, they believe that it is necessary to have sex in order to feel what is like being into someone else's shoes. In their mind; an intimate, profound and symbiotic relation between two individuals cannot happen at an intellectual level, but only by having sex.

I only hope the New World Order is inevitable just because our planet has been secretly taken over by aliens, which the UN is just trying to keep calm and see how best humans can negotiate with them. Actually, I have to be honest, I wouldn't mind them.

I already feel an alien in Italy, which makes Italians alien to me as much as I might be one to them. Furthermore, while living in the U.S., I was always considered a legal alien by the law, therefore I couldn't but look forward to having real alien neighbors.

I only hope it's not an alien intelligence behind all my life, manipulating my existence to achieve their goals on Earth and, above anything else, I really hope it's not aliens making sure I get no pussy, so they can have their private sex guinea pig.

Or may be it's just the Pope who doesn't want me to get laid, as I should only fuck to procreate. However, I am fine with that too. I mean, I have no problems getting laid and flood a pussy with my sperm without even warring if I'll end up with a kid or not.

Now, I know someone may think that my obsessions with someone secretly ensuring I don't get laid is just the proof I am in reality just an homophobic, repressed homosexual who is trying to hide from his own real sexual identity. However, I am fucking straight!

As a matter of fact, I have also been a strong activist of gay rights, and truly hope the New World Order is going to promote a more righteous environment for gays as well. I couldn't wish getting laid so badly preventing others from having the very same desire.

I wish the New World Order granted everybody the right of getting laid, for sake of one's psychological hygiene. I don't see why a State should grant medical treatment to those in need, ignoring the sick people like me, who are so desperately in need of pussy.

It's just a pussy that I need. A simple fucking pussy. I am not asking for a ride on the moon, or a visit to the international space station after all. It's just like a wheelchair; if one needs it, means it is necessary, or I'll rather go horse riding than wheel chairing.

I do not even want to believe the New World Order is unable to fix all Earth's problems at once. I understand that's challenging and very difficult to accomplish because of the overall, still largely diffused ignorance around the globe, yet surely very possible.

I am sure that if all of Earth's problems were resolved, I would get my pussy without problems happily ever after. Therefore, fucking world, get the fuck out of your nasty ghettos, caves and hiding nests and start figuring out the best way to solve our problems.

If another war is really necessary to end this shit on the planet; well, let's be it. I am surely going to be getting more pussy in war times than I am during peace time like now. Plus, mercenaries are granted, here and there, special deals in terms of pussy benefits.

For instance, from all the time I have wasted in my life studying the arguments of those anti New World Order movements, and informing others on the issues, I have not even gotten a single pussy in return. I mean, not even my hands on a pair of boobs.

Fuck them. Fuck those fucking Arab-like, mafia pseudo-terrorists who don't even fucking understand that a clitoris is much funnier than a fucking stupid penis, and fucking men are by nature inferior than women, as they are the child bearers in the human race.

Today I received a bad news from one of the cruise lines I applied for. Luckily enough, I sent my resume to a couple more as well. Life goes by day by day at this point, and I take it as it comes. Warring is useless, and it only makes things worse and harder.

Sometimes, I still ask myself what my life would have been right now, hadn't I been so rude with my publisher, Publish America in Maryland. They gave me a chance, yet I wasn't able to handle the stress of an FBI arrest and being kicked out of college at once.

I still wonder how different my writings could have been, had I entrusted Publish America my works and inspiration, instead of literally telling them to fuck off. Too often one treats his or her only friends the worst, instead of cherishing them the most.

However, afterwards is always too late. As they say, once you go black, you never go back. I'm fucked now, I can't even go back to Publish America asking them to forgive me and handling them all my books, as I am no longer a U.S. legal resident either.

I made some very big mistakes in my life. However, I can only look back and say I have learned my lessons well. No matter what, had I not done everything I did in my past life, I would have never gotten here where I am now, despite I don't like it here.

In a way, had I liked it more back there and then, I wouldn't have been right here right now. Saying I don't like my life right now, and judging everything else accomplished previously, I can only say to be the only sole responsible for my destiny and fate.

It is inevitable that one's life must take into consideration how it affects others. Perhaps, that's just what I lacked. Despite always trying to follow the law, my impetus may have caused lots of harm onto others, and I should have considered that, despite being legal.

The law cannot take care of everyone and everything as parents do, and I hope the New World Order will improve the understanding among the public of the maturity necessary to live up to the 21st century challenges, as human beings fully conscious of their limits.

Potential itself means really nothing if it is not properly oriented toward benefiting humanity as a whole. Perhaps, if I am still alive today, it's just because of the bona fide or good faith I put in all my actions and interactions with others, despite they often abuse it.

After all, there is still one law governing the universe as we know it, affirming that for every little action there is a reaction. Just as the ancient Romans used to say, you know when that time comes and it is necessary to unleash the dogs; and that's always war.

I would like for the New World Order not to have to come into existence by mean of another big war; however, it may be just necessary and inevitable. It's a law of the universe, and nobody can do anything against the power of nature and the universe itself.

Perhaps, I have always been scared about the New World Order, only because unconsciously I have always known that when such times arise, it is always going to be hell on Earth. With the worsening of the economy and terrorism, that time has come.

I am afraid I'll have to learn how to get by without job and income. I don't have to worry about food and shelter, and that's already a great accomplishment. But that's just like any poor people living thanks to charity organizations, such as the Knights of Malta.

I would have never thought I had needed their hospitality and solidarity one day. I no longer have the strength to fight political battle such us the one against the governor of Italy's central bank, whereas I demanded an income as my mathematical right.

You see, when one like me tries all possible venues in order to deliver a message, or to create a bridge across people who are only apparently unwilling to listen to your motivations; then, one like me, has the God given right to start a war to preserve himself.

What I am saying is always the same story. Once the mob deprives me from having an income, then I also become sexually deprived. And once I become sexually deprived, you're fucking around with the God given, natural reproduction instinct of a human being.

Almost all across Europe and the United States, the concept of a guaranteed minimum income is starting to become much diffused. We must thank Thomas Paine for that, who first started to promote it in his "Capital grants provided at the age of majority" in 1795.

- 123 -

In fact, just as Shakespeare looked back at Roman classics for inspiration, so did Paine. Therefore, the minimum guaranteed income is nothing more but the old Roman concept of salary, when salt was distributed to the population free for everybody.

Interesting enough, the only ones not benefiting from a minimum guaranteed salary are mafia affiliates and terrorists, who would lose their economical domination and grip over the population or general public, once they were granted a new purchasing power.

Also, the concept of a minimum guaranteed income has nothing to do with communism either. In fact, it will foremost advantage capitalism, by increasing consumers' purchasing power. I already explained and revealed the mathematical foundations behind it.

From a criminology standpoint, not only a minimum guaranteed salary is the best remedy against all mobs, but for public health as well, a minimum guaranteed salary represents a financial stress relief and the possibility of paying for cures when necessary.

All I ever wanted to do with my political activism was to propose a deal or contract to the New World Order, which would establish a new era by putting in place a new socio-economical agreement benefiting both consumers and capitalists at the same time.

Of course, I'd be lying if I denied I'd be the first one benefiting from such a deal. I mean, can you imagine how different my life would be if I could have my own place and not having to worry about living under my fucking stupid mother's same roof?

Now, a minimum guaranteed salary would also benefit minorities such as people with disabilities and women and general too. The latter always being mistreated by preventing them from having an income, therefore deprived of their freedom and independence.

I am not interested in decanting love and romanticism at all. I'd rather decant sex and eroticism, because that's always been women's only natural possibility for protest. I write to defend women's rights as human beings, not only lovers and mothers.

I might even be getting some pussy for that after all; you never know. However, I am a very romantic lover; despite I have never known what women really thought about me from that prospective. Though, I am sure if one treats women right, they will do the same.

Ironically speaking, I am not only so lonely physically and morally, but also according the personal data registry, I am the only person named Rinaldo Pilla in the whole fucking planet. I mean, I am going fucking extinct here. Now, that's fucking scarry.

I wouldn't mind to impregnate a couple thousand pussies just to make sure I didn't go extinct for real. That's just my natural reaction to such possibility. I mean, if one doesn't want to die, must have children; there are no other ways but reproduction.

Unfortunately, as for every good deal, it is not possible that only one part contributes to the agreement. Therefore, for the New World Order to function properly, a minimum guaranteed salary must be balanced by eradication of tax evasion and black labor.

So, once again, I feel hammered between these two contrasting forces, which if not balanced, will inevitably conduct to war. I pay the price of sexual and financial constrictions only because the mob does not want to give up its control over the black market.

On the other hand, banks and capitalists do not want to grant a minimum guaranteed salary as, in the absence of even more severe controls to prevent tax evasion and black market, it will only make things much worse and actually score only in terrorists' favor.

Just like Pope Julius II tormented Michelangelo, so I have been persecuted by a material, earthly power trying to buy my soul for money. I like money; however, I am not willing to give up my soul for it, and I'd rather live poor if I could not have both.

I hope Pope Francis I will hear my call, and answer it to the benefit of the New World Order, making sure nobody will lose from its establishment, particularly the Holy Roman Catholic Church. I truly believe an new age is possible, without even fighting.

Had I to choose a number, because I was born in 1977, and having the Black Death lasted 7 years in Venafro, my number would be 777. That's my lucky number, and I don't care what it means in Jewish numerology or in the Neapolitan cabala known as smorfia.

No matter what, I'd rather look at the New World Order as a comedy than a tragedy, as too often its opponents depict it. In a way, that's just nothing more than my philosophy of life, whereas I always try to have a positive attitude rather than a negative one.

I also wonder if, just as Garibaldi has been called "Hero of Two Worlds," I'll ever be called "Poet of the Two Worlds." I only hope such recognition comes within my lifetime, so that I'll have one more chance to return to the United States as a crowned VIP.

About six months ago, at new year's eve, I was able to exchange a few lines with a Mexican American Playmate named Raquel Pomplun[2], who actually just became Playmate of the year. Couldn't help but think that Garibaldi married a Brazilian, Anita.

Therefore, Italian strong attraction for American women in general is nothing new. However, I must say to prefer women from the United States, rather than from the Americas in general. I even told Raquel to come visit Venafro, which may never happen though.

Another very important thing I hope for the New World Order to accomplish is investigating more the secrets of longevity, such as for the French supercentenarian Jeanne Louise Calment, who lived 122 years and 164 days, in order to stretch lifespan even more.

In my opinion, modern Italians are not living up to the expectations of their predecessors. Or perhaps it's just that I am an irreducible nostalgic. No matter how, none of the great Italian poets would recognize themselves in the current Italian society.

Nevertheless, one of Venafro's most outstanding natives was just Leopoldo Pilla, an Italian geologist and politician who lost his life during the First Italian War of Independence in 1848, between the Kingdom of Sardinia and the Austrian Empire.

---

2 Playboy Magazine U.S., Vol. 60, No. 5 - June 2013. Playmate of the year, pp. 116.

It may be just a coincidence I am a Pilla as well, and that Garibaldi is buried in Sardinia, and that I am afraid of earthquakes, despite Venafro being of very high seismic risk due to its position right on the edge of both the Eurasian and African fault.

However, with such prestigious predecessors, how could I really ever join the anti New World Order supporters? I am afraid if I did that, the soul of Leopoldo Pilla would cause a earthquake to make sure I don't ruin the overall reputation of the Pillas in the world.

As if that wasn't already enough, I'll have to face the anger of another great poet, Giacomo Leopardi, whose tombstone is also located at the Parco Virgiliano, or Park of Remembrance, next to Virgil. Leopardi loved Pilla, as he used to call his sister Paolina.

I can't find any other explanation why Giacomo Leopardi would have called his sister Pilla, if not that he was referring to Leopoldo Pilla. Nevertheless, Paolina, a.k.a. Pilla, was responsible for several French translations and a biography of Mozart as well.

Now, this is the heavy cultural heritage and burden I carry with me throughout life. Anyhow, what really disgusts me, is that I must say it in English, as Italians are so indifferent to me, and actually seem wanting to repress, silence and hide my story at any costs.

Had it not been for my sick father, I would have never resisted living in Italy. I feel there is nothing I can do for this country, in order to help its destiny. I surely do not want end up dead like Leopolodo for a bunch of fucking ignorant and idiot pseudo-Arabs.

May be they are afraid I would be just too influential on the public, because of my personal familial history and historical relevance. Nevertheless, as Machiavelli said, every people have the ruler they deserve and Italy's republican experience is still too fragile.

That's why I can honestly say to have felt really at home only the United States. I feel in exile living in Italy, not at home at all. That's why I have also sent my resume to Playboy, in Los Angeles, California. There is no other place I can call home but the US.

I feel more like an observer here in Venafro than anything else. I see only shit in front of me, despite I have done everything possible to help improving the living conditions. I ran for Major, contacted UNESCO, and promoted the city any possible way.

The truth is that these local people are just too ignorant at this point in time. They are primitive as any far isolated African tribes may be in the middle of the Congolese jungle. Well, let's not talk about Congo, as my second cousin may hear me mention it.

I really have nobody else in life other than my father. My brother does not even speak English, and he is culturally very comfortable with Italians, not like me. I guess that's why he chose not to go to school, just get his high school diploma, and become a cop instead.

As far as my mothers goes; well, I am afraid I have already wasted way too much time mentioning her in my writings. I have another cousin, the only son of my father's brother living in Fermo, not too far from Giacomo Leopardi place of birth either.

However, he does not speak English either, therefore we can only communicate in Italian, and that's way too limiting from my point of view. My great grandfather Angelo Maria Pilla is buried in the States, but as far as I know, there are no living heirs.

Perhaps my real problem is being a cosmopolitan, globalized citizen already, and that may be just too ahead of times. So, even when criticizing NATO's defense policies or U.S. and EU monetary policies, it was always with a globalized personality.

I can honestly say that, within the NATO block, the EU has still many problems ahead to face before being able to fully contribute to the North Atlantic Alliance more efficiently, stably and securely, in order to accelerate its people's progress as well.

I can't believe the lack of pussy would have ever gotten me so far as writing so much and so openly about these issues once again. I guess I must look for a NATO babe rather than just a simple American or European one, as we may be just more compatible.

In a way, I envision the New World Order as allowing for NATO to develop even better commercial relations within its borders as it has happened for Europe since the end of WWII. A common North Atlantic market may also be the solution to the economical crisis.

And, if there is market, there is fish for sale; hoping it won't go all extinct before the New World Order actually gets into place. And, if there is fish for sale on the market, somewhere out there, is room for my swordfish as well, meaning dipping my dick in a pussy.

New World Order simply means endless possibilities, which have not been written yet. Attributing it a negative connotation without giving it a chance is as discriminatory as an act of ignorance may be toward any human being, of any sex, race and religion.

Crazy Italian people actually domesticate chickens to stalk their neighbors. I had never seen that before, despite I knew of cockfights, which I believe being an Arab tradition. That may be why raising chickens is not allowed within American city limits.

They do that as complementary to domesticating crows for the very same purpose of stalking people. It's just that this Arab-like, mafioso culture is really incompatible with true Italian culture and heritage, as expressed artistically throughout the centuries.

As a matter of fact, I have come to understand that such artistic achievements in Italy are explained by Italy's very simple endless conflict with this mafia-like, pseudo-Arabic culture infecting the Nation. As a matter of fact, art is Italy's immune response to that.

In a way, now that this mafia-like, Islamic terrorist subculture has infected not only America, but the rest of the world as well, I hope for Italy's natural antibodies and experience to be helpful by transferring such antibodies to the New World Order.

I hope to have accomplished just that with my artistic and poetical endeavors. I don't feel just an Italian or American artist, as that would be too constraining to me. I feel a global citizen, therefore a global artist welcoming critiques, but not any illegal behaviors.

I am intolerant of this fucking mafioso, gangster or even mobster culture which has now spread all over within the NATO block, therefore no longer just a phenomenon confined within Italy's borders. It influences my sexual and financial sphere too much.

I am already way too fucking disgusted by own mother who once said to be supportive of the mafioso ghetto culture. I mean, I am fucking disgusted by own mother and the environment I was born in. That's pretty fucking heavy to deal with in the first place.

I couldn't but find shelter within the English language. I don't give a fuck about the Italian language at all; Dante, Boccaccio, and all Italian poets in general. I am fucking disgusted by Italian culture to the point I completely deny having ever had anything to do with it.

I am a way, it was hard for me, coming from the Old Word, to integrate in the New World; that being the Unites States. The New World Order is nothing more but a necessary attempt to fill this gap which has been creating over time between the two continents.

NATO faces this difficult challenge of bridging such cultural gap in order to gain always larger public support, and understanding of its core values, mission and its absolutely necessary role in defending today's Western interests and security in the world.

With intelligence comes progress; however, with progress comes responsibility. Unwillingness to face up to the challenges of the future is like dining the benefits so far achieved along the way. One may be tired of the long journey; however, it never ends.

Rest along the way is not only necessary but strongly recommended. How will the New World Order educate the future citizens of the planet is a difficult task for me to even imagine. Global Media are reality, but Governments lack true commitment.

When politicians talk about the treat of populism, despite they don't say it openly; they are referring to overall ignorance of the masses. Even Pope Benedict XVI publicly reported that the social gap created with scientific progress may be risky for democracy.

I hope for the New World Order, together with other world leaders from the religious, scientific, political and art arena, to be able to fill such gap, and better educate people in order to overcome such a difficult socio-economical moment and phase worldwide.

Headed toward my fifth year of sexual abstinence, I got a closer understanding of the ancient Greek myth of love, according to which there were three sexes; males, females, and androgens. Androgens being the asexual beings the other sexes derived from.

Now, trying to analyze and compare ancient Greek sexuality to modern, one can soon notice the absence of transsexuals, due to the absence of medical advancements. Also, gays were included in those two sexual categories, independently of their genitals.

In fact, because gays had specific sexual needs and desires, they were considered either male or female, depending for example on their role-play in the couple sexual life. For instance, and active male gay may have considered male, while a passive one a female.

Nevertheless, what is most important, is that the concept of and androgen was that of a superior, more mystical nature; just as of today's priesthood or novitiate, so openly defined by their vows of abstinence. That's nothing like my forced, prolonged abstinence.

In fact, because of abstinence, I have gotten a change to understand vaguely what they feel with a complete sexless life. Just as for gays sex didn't matter, but just their role-play in the couple, so androgens are complete sexual beings filling vacancies with faith.

I couldn't know how to explain what being a priest or a nun may be as of nowadays, despite psychologically may be nothing different compared to the androgens of ancient Greek, and despite today's dogma and Great Mystery of the faith is different.

What I know for sure is that I could never take a vow of abstinence for sure. I mean, it has already been very hard living without a pussy for almost five years now. However, without masturbating I could have never survived all the stress I had to face those days.

The same is for monks, just as for priests and nuns, who also take the vows of sexual abstinence. Now, that kind of choice has nothing really to do with one being straight or gay, I believe. I guess, it really is a matter of having a true calling or vocation.

The way I feel about it, that's also how one should look at the Ancient Greek aphorism "Know thyself," found at the temple of Apollo at Delphi. Ancient people used to go to such temple looking for the oracles, yet they were welcomed with that phrase.

Truth really lies within us, in a very sacred mental stage. Truth is a state of mind, and if only one can reach it within himself or herself, there will be no more reason for fearing the future or our existence, so that an oracle or magician won't even be needed in the future.

The only problem being that I know myself pretty well by now, and hope to have been able to prove it in writing, as I have unleashed my psyche loose into my sheets. I just keep on writing every day a little bit more out of boringness and loneliness.

The hardest thing one may face looking for himself or herself is just the fear of loneliness which affects all human beings. In fact, I am still dealing with the idea I may have to abandon myself to the idea of having to spend the rest of my life alone, as I am right now.

Keep dreaming for things to change is absolutely righteous and human; however, I should be prepared to the idea that getting even older and penniless, things are not going to improve for me in any way. I might as well just best prepare to face such possible reality.

In fact, I might never be able to leave Italy again, therefore I should get used to the idea of accepting the fact I must somehow deal with such possibility. In a way, it's about time for me to start thinking about a plan B, given that my words may remain silent.

Some days I am so bored, I don't even feel like masturbating. Today for instance, I quit smoking, so I am even more bored than usual. Now, I don't want to give the impression I spend my days doing nothing at all, it's just that for my age I could be doing more.

Perhaps, the fact I write is just mere coincidence. In fact, had the unemployment rate not been so high in Italy right now, probably I would have never been writing this book. No matter what, it's just that on top of it all, I am unemployed, single, lonely and broke.

I am not even sure writing this book out of boringness will be of any help selling it. The fact being that every paragraph I add is the result of the money and the time I saved by not smoking tobacco, but also the necessity to spend such time somehow.

The city is hostile to me, mostly due to my lawsuit against my mother's relatives, that almost the entire city seems to know about; despite they say absolutely nothing to me. So, I feel constantly stalked by a lack of privacy while I walk through Venafro.

I guess sitting in my office in the basement is like hiding in a bunker. I only get disturbed when my mother, as rudely as she is, slams the door of the upstairs apartment. I can't really do anything if they are so rude and it's too late for them to change their ways.

Once again, the only redundant and recurring thought I have, is getting the fuck out of this place as soon as possible, and stop giving a shit about my sick father. They have money and a pension, yet too mean to hire a caretaker, while I am stuck here.

I am afraid my mother is starting to worry what will happen to her when she gets older, as she is now spending almost all her time with my father, taking care of him. I only hope she won't get sick after him as well. However, she has a pension as my father.

For some strange and to me unknown reason, they reject the possibility of spending their retirement at an elder or care home. I guess their culture is still too tight to their home in order to even be considering possible, more practical and affordable alternatives.

Of course, those are things one cannot decide overnight, and they should be considered slowly throughout the course of one's life. However, Italians are so stubborn that don't seem able to look at real estate as a simple consumer good, to be changed at any time.

Do I sound too picky? Is it why I cannot get laid? Is it because I think too much? What the fuck is wrong with this people? I refuse thinking there is anything wrong with me, until someone tells me that. The problem is that I am being just completely ignored.

It is like everybody knows me, yet nobody really wants to have anything to do with me. And I can obviously understand why, as I have been always honest about how I fell about Italians. However, I was only able to be assaulted by my mother's relatives.

Unfortunately, they are very ignorant people as well. None of them went to university, therefore they knowledge of the world is strongly conditioned by popular beliefs rather than factual convictions. It is in stagnant moments like this that I hate my life.

If I don't get a job on a cruise ship, I'll always be able to look at immigrating to Australia. Over there seems employers are looking for skilled workers and professionals from all over the world. The problem is what kind of job should I be trying to get in Australia?

The funny thing is that, not even a month ago, I went at the U.S. Consulate in Naples to get my last will notarized. As I wrote in my last wishes, I left everything to the U.S. Federal Government. There I saw a nice international affairs employee I wished dating.

I am afraid going back to the United States would still be a little difficult for me, I am not sure. I left with unpaid student loans, and that's why I made sure to indicate the Government as beneficiary in my last will. At least, they are gonna get all the bullshit I wrote.

Once one is deprived of his or her own independence, beginning with the financial one, everything else is just bullshit. I actually feel for the people out there who are in much worse situations than mine. In reality, I know these are rough times for everybody.

In a way, I willingly took on the hard task of writing the story of my times, as I have been able to witness many realities, due to my previous extensive traveling and life experiences abroad. Having lost all that diversity and stimuli I was used to is hard to accept.

Venafro was just not ready for me when I landed here. I have always tried to respect other people's dignity before deciding it was time to end that false, so-called respectability and just start being me instead, careless about others' opinions and judgments.

I believe to have been the cause of a local cultural shock across the community, as much as they have been a complete reject immune response for me. I am afraid I wakened the sleeping beauty from her sleep and dreams, throwing reality straight at her face.

I no longer even look to be accepted by the local community or wish for them to take anything good from me. It's just that either they get I am here and cannot go anywhere else, or I'll start fucking reporting everyone to the police, till they put me in jail.

I am afraid the same story I have experienced in Davenport is once again repeating itself in Venafro as well. Now, I can admit having my shares of responsibility, as I am not insane. However, what the fuck, can it all be just a coincidence? I don't belive it is.

I am afraid having been used for a larger, broader, international investigation, covering crossing areas of reciprocal interests between the United States and Italy. In a way, I was the perfect pretext for such an international investigation, or may be not.

It is possible that everything started because someone suspected me being an international wine smuggler, who may have been smuggling much more than just alcohol, hiding behind the cartel of his own international business. The idea is actually pretty scary.

As a matter of fact, last time I had sex was right before I was arrested by the FBI in Davenport, Iowa. I wonder if I am still under investigation, especially because I also sent them a tip in regard of local Italian politicians doing business with companies in Panama.

The fact is I always trusted justice and law and order enforcement agencies. I just don't know what the heck I may have hacked or tapped into, but it has got to be something huge, and perhaps I even accidentally just hit the largest money laundering apparatus.

Perhaps, the reason of all my troubles is being kind of a ganja guru. I have never really shined away from my passion for the cannabis plant. I am not just a stoner, but a true scientist when it comes down to cannabis. I am truly fascinated by that plant.

But I don't live in Amsterdam, Madrid or California, therefore I can't even recall last time I smoked some hashish here in Venafro, as weed is much harder to find. Cannabis psychoactive properties taught me a lot about the human brain, especially my synapses.

Together with wine, cannabis contributed to the development of my sexual understanding. Despite I don't really know what any of my lovers ever thought about me in bed, rather than a comment by one of them once, saying I was stallion; I may be a horrible lover.

Anyway, I couldn't but hope for the New World Order to decriminalize the use of recreational cannabis within the NATO block, while focusing a bit more on the new synthetic drugs, which I fear being much more dangerous than good old weed.

The same I wish for prostitution being regulated, allowing it when one is of a certain mature age, such as twenty-seven, and ensuring medical checkups and taxes for the oldest job on Earth. I hope for future generations to avoid my mistakes, and enjoy life even more.

As far as marijuana, the thing about that plant and its psychoactive cannabinoid compounds, is that as all things affecting the brain, being very cautious couldn't but be an imperative must. Because taboos are much worse than sun burns, I decided to study the plant.

I am not just referring to a botanical standpoint, but at neurological levels, in terms of how cannabis affects and influences the human brain and perceptions. I have almost always used marijuana by myself, despite interacting with other people regardless.

What is sure about cannabis or marijuana is that it enhances one's natural neurons capability to fire the synapses. This does not make one more intelligent or anything like that, just makes the cannabis user differently receptive of its environmental surroundings.

I have always felt marijuana has the ability to enhance interpersonal communication capabilities, particularly telepathy. Over time, that hypothesis has proven true for me. I cannot say having conducted a true medical and scientific research though.

I don't think marijuana has developed my natural telepathic abilities, but just refined them. Actually, I know for fact that, when I use marijuana, my telepathic capacities are largely increased, and people around me react and respond as they perceived it.

I think my cannabis use may also have influenced some of my relationships. In fact, I am afraid women feel much more vulnerable when I use marijuana, in terms of their diminished privacy due to my physical presence and encephalic interaction.

In a way, telepathy may represent a treat to women, due to the already acclaimed male physical advantage. I am afraid women have felt very scared and threatened by my telepathic capabilities, especially when under the effect of cannabis and around them.

Not that I have ever been violent or disrespectful while high on cannabis; in fact, I actually only get sillier and mellower when I am high, despite that's just a consequence of all the things I end up thinking about while high. Yet there is a big risk I see.

In fact, the problem is not cannabis itself, but who uses it. Due to marijuana's natural ability to facilitate telepathy, it's greatly possible that criminal minds or terrorist may want to use it in order to coerce and manipulate their chosen victims' brains.

In fact, there is nothing easier than plagiarizing a person while using marijuana. When one is high on marijuana, his or her brain becomes just as an antenna, capable or receiving encephalic signals by nearby brains and vice versa. It literally opens a channel.

Upon this communicative channel being created or open between two individuals while high on cannabis, it is possible to transfer images and emotions telepathically from one brain to another, therefore from one individual to another, just as imagists poets do.

That's the greatest opportunity to plagiarize another person's brain right there, at your finger tips. Cannabis is a great catalyst for plagiarism, especially if those willing to take control over another person's brain and emotions use spiritualism to plagiarize.

It is much easier to plagiarize another person's brain using fear created by a mixture of hallucinogenic images associated to very deep spiritual feelings, especially if those relate to the idea or experience of death. That is sufficient to frighten a person for life.

In reality, that's what voodoo is really about, and too many fools ended up believing its crap unfortunately. Most of the time this bad influencing becomes stalking, as it continues throughout the life of the person whose brain has been hacked so to speak.

Now, is marijuana itself responsible for that? No, not at all. The cannabis plant is not a mean one, or it has any possibility of influencing what the user's experience might be. It's the user who really makes a difference. I am a cannabis guru just by knowing it.

In my case, my brain's telepathic capabilities started to develop well before I even started using weed. In a way, telepathy is just a very basic, primordial ability of any brains, human as well as animal. Studying really forged my mind and my telepathic skills.

Once again, under the effect of cannabis, a brain naturally enters a certain telepathic state. However, if one's brain is not strong enough, as for education and schooling, it can easily be plagiarized by those willing to take control over a person's life and brain.

I am afraid being so telepathic that, despite being in Venafro, as soon as I look at a photo of a model in Los Angels, I can connect with her, as if I had her phone number. Now, that is pretty scary for a woman, and threatening for the police and law enforcement.

Once again I went to Mount Holy Cross and threw a magnolia seed by the ruins of an ancient wall that I believe used to take all the way to the Norman tower above. While on Mount Holy Cross, one must be always careful and aware of the vipers that live there.

As a matter of fact, today I just realized that the snake is a common symbol in medicine for the very simple reason that as one must be cold blooded in the presence of vipers for example, so doctors must preserve the exact same attitude when treating patients.

The most difficult thing to accomplish in imagist poetry is the fusion of emotions and thoughts connected to such emotions, so that readers can then recreate the exact image of what is being described, wih no possibility of misinterpreting the whole message.

In a way, the fact I love being outdoor is intrinsically connected to another old Latin quotation stating, "mens sana in corpore sano." In English, that translates as healthy mind in a healthy body, and as far as I am concerned, that's the very principle of telepathy itself.

Just as France boycotted Joan of Arc; as Rome boycotted Scipio Africanus, to the point he deliberately took the way of exile completely disgusted of his homeland; so I, before being boycotted by Italy, anticipating my destiny, boycott Italy voluntarily.

Just as Scipio Africanus ordered having an inscription on his tomb saying, "ungrateful homeland, you will not even have my bones," so I ask the United States to became a U.S. citizen, as I do not want to die as Italian citizen, even if I'll end up being buried in Italy.

I don't want to have anything to do with this pseudo-Arab like culture which pretends being Italian on my homeland. I reject all that fucking pseudo-Arab bullshit from my own Italian heritage, which I have boycotted because of its inability to do the same.

Italians are double faced, European and African at their convenience. I am surely not African, or even European at this point of my life, as a true unified Europe does not really exist yet. I am simply American, as I belong to the New World, not the Old.

The Old World is dead, as far as I am concerned. People may try to oppose the truth as much as they want, however there is no way back to barbarism in the 21st century. The New World Order is not a matter of a conspiracy theory, but an evolving political scenario.

These fucking Italians are so stupid they spend their entire existence thinking about they day they are going to day. It is just if the fear for the 2012 Maya end of the world has never ended here in Italy. They are just insane in my opinion, or schizophrenics.

They are very irrational; therefore, they start panicking instead of finding logic and reasonable ways to fix their problems. I only now understand what always gets Italy into conflicts and crisis every so often. They are so genetically related that are schizophrenics.

At first, I didn't understand why French President Nicolas Sarkozy was suggesting French people to intermix with foreigners. However, after having come back from America, I understand his point pretty clearly now, and couldn't even agree more.

I feel like people in the Old World have really been closely interbreeding for too long, to the point they present less genetical variation compared to people in the New World. And I am not even talking about interracial unions, just broader selection ranges.

Perhaps, the issue is not even genetically related as much as culturally. After all, I was born by two Italian parents; therefore, I am genetically a full blood Italian. However, having lived in America, and exposed to different cultures changed my life.

So, one can say that, being America the melting pot of the world, what that is teaching us is important for the progress of Europe and the rest of the world as well. Ironically speaking, Italians live in a very different, self inflicted and freely chosen apartheid system.

They are so primitive and rude, especially in the south, that after a while it becomes almost impossible to keep one's mental sanity due to all the environmental and noise pollution they make in order to keep living undisturbed, as if the rest of the world didn't exist.

Being very telepathic makes things much worse. They try any possible way to disturb me from writing, by honking horns by my house all the time; my neighbors slamming their garage doors, as well as my own fucking mother always being noisy upstairs.

I mean, I am thinking and writing in English, while out there in Venafro, all others are not even speaking Italian, but their horrible Arab-like dialect which not even the young generation knows or is willing to use anymore. They can't stand times have changed.

In fact, the local people in Venafro cannot even stand people from Naples, which is not even a couple of hours away. Venafro is just nothing but a fucking ghetto. The inhabitants of Venafro in fact are proud not to be speaking the Neapolitan dialect, but their own.

I feel like being in kindergarten with these people. Not only Italy is a young and still very fragile Republic, but Italians as a whole are very immature human beings, as they have not fully embraced a national unitary identity yet, and still think as in separate tribes.

I hope the New World Order is an opportunity for Italy and Italians, as for the rest of likeminded people around the globe, to wake up to the challenges without wasting any time. In a globalized world there is no room for tribalism and barbarism.

I guess, had I been able to live by myself, I wouldn't have been so stressed out as I am right now. For instance, just the fact that every time I hear my mother talking, she reminds me of a ravening crow, and that's driving me crazy. Once again, that's just money talks.

The more days go by, the less chances I get to get laid. The situation is really driving me toward the edge of a cliff. Nothing seems to be changing anytime soon, or I don't have the impression anything good can happen staying right here in fucking Venafro.

I can't even roll a cigarette either, as I don't have the money to buy tobacco. Actually, I don't mind staying away from tobacco either, as I don't think that smoking all that much, just to keep my mind busy doing something, is very healthy for me in the first place.

I am afraid I'll have to stop reading Playboy as well, due to the fact that the magazine may actually be just over stimulating my expectations, distracting me from just focusing and catching reality. I know very well I am not going to meet any Playmate.

Once, a girl I used to know form my childhood told me that I was too goodhearted as I was born in the wrong period. At that time, I told her I didn't think so. However, it's possible she was right. Anyhow, I really enjoyed my life up to about five years ago.

My problems started when I went to New York on TV for the first time. Ever since, my life has not been the same. First I had some problems with my computer at home in Davenport, right after I came back from New York and even reported that to the police.

Actually, two years I think to have accidentally hacked into the Davenport police informatics system; I was arrested by the FBI, kicked out of college, and no way left but moving back to fucking Italy. At times, I really wished I had been killed in the States.

I understood right away that my life back in Italy was going to be difficult, as people here were too ignorant and I didn't have those kinds of good connections which may have introduced me to the upper or middle class Italian social environment. That was right.

Basically, I moved from the ghetto in Davenport to the ghetto in Venafro. Comparing ghettos, I must honestly say and admit my ghetto in Davenport was far more attractive than fucking Venafro. At least, I had a much diverse variety of pussy to look at there.

Once back in Italy, and well settled in the ghetto in Venafro, I started sending my resume to basically all major Italian companies I could possible get a hold of. Completely ignored by all of them, not a single company ever sent me a rejection letter either.

At that point I decided to run for Major of the ghetto, in Venafro. I figured the pay wouldn't have been so bad after all, and the job would have lasted for five years. Enough for some tickets to go on vacation once in a while, and may be even get laid here and there.

However, that was not meant to be for me either. That's why I decided my Italian citizenship is worth just as much as fucking toilette paper. I don't need it, as I am not planning on using my political rights in Italy ever again, to represent chimpanzees.

I keep writing only because I don't know what else to do instead, as I already gave up smoking. This fucking ghetto is ruled by chimps and their hypocrisy. Their real condition, and all their attempts at covering it, creates the deception of the ghetto.

They hate me not because I take their women, or because I take their jobs away. They hate me because I tell the truth, which they do not want to hear. They would rather keep sleeping and pretending I and the rest of the world didn't exist, but surrendering.

So, here I am. I was hated in Davenport, and am hated in Venafro too. Actually, also Garibaldi, Hero of the Two Worlds, was not loved by everyone either. Perhaps that's how visionaries are normally treated by their contemporaries; but that fucking sucks.

Well, at least Garibaldi not only used to get laid, but was actually granted accommodation, food and all the benefits of being a soldier; by his friendly line, of course. I get food and shelter, but that's by my fucking mother, whom I can't fucking stand either.

In a way, in order to coexist with my mother, I had to learn the manners of the ghetto. In fact, when I see her I pretend I tolerate her, while in all reality I can't fucking stand her. After all, that's how everybody lives here in the ghetto, as well as elsewhere's.

I guess, once you are born in the ghetto, you'll either spend all your life trying to escape, or die in it. I can only hope for the New World Order to be a world without ghettos. I may never see that day, as I may die in the ghetto; however, I did not belong here.

I am afraid I might have to just fucking end this book right here. I don't think anything is ever going to change anyway. The longer I keep writing, the more bored I become. Writing may be just a double-bladed sword as well, and it would be better that way.

I don't think I have much to add anyway. I am just going to have to learn how to watch TV instead of writing. Plus, nobody will ever know how my story really ended and no matter what, good wine is always to be found in small barrels, just like this book.

I hope having decanted my disgust for the Old World fairly enough, in order to justify my decision to support the New World Order, despite having previously strongly criticized it. Critics are legitimate, but recognitions and acknowledgments mandatory.

Just like my life, my writing was rough and casual at first; then, it finally came together as a revelation. And just as Virgil in the Aeneid, so I tried to personify the poetical and lyric spirit which was often referred to as "muse" in the Ancient World.

Just like the Ancient World is no longer, so the Old World is vanished as well. The New World simply represents the new wine; the last come. The New World Order is nothing but a physiological attempt by the system to confront with such new reality.

Just like the Roman goddess Diana, which in Latin meant heavenly or divine, and who swore never to marry; so I have been a hunter under many aspects. I have been hunting down myself during all my life, nailing it down everywhere I found it.

Just like Diana, who is often represented with her arrows and a deer, so I have had a pen and deer-like spirit on Earth. As deer must stay always alert to spot any sign of treat in the woods, so I had to be constantly vigilant of my surroundings to stay alive.

For sure, other than being inspired by ancient Roman poetry, without even considering Arab literature like the One Thousand and One Nights; I wanted to recreate the feeling of a Northern minstrel, skald or scold, just like in the Old English poem Beowulf.

Despite not writing a play for Queen Elizabeth II, like Shakespeare used to do for Queen Elizabeth I; I still hope having honored her attempting to make English my own, as if I were a reptile, able to change skin on demand, or just a soldier wearing camouflage.

After doubting the magnanimity and nobility of Her Majesty, I cannot but admit and realize her good faith in supporting the New World Order too, for the good of her very fellow subjects, as well as the rest of the citizens of the planet, no matter where they live.

As a matter of fact, I would like to be remembered not as much as Poet of the Two Worlds as Poet of the New World Order. After all the negative things written about this inevitable and upcoming era, I want to be the first one to have ever decanted it in poetry.

Who knows, I might even ending up getting some New World Order pussy afterwards. Unfortunately, there is nothing I can do in order to keep my mind off the subject. Just like women's curves, life is a rollercoaster, with only one possibility to hit the bow.

I must also admit writing just as I fuck. Well, that's given I still remember how to. Anyway, at first I am always nervous with any new chick, as they are all virgins before me. Not that I expect them to be virgin, but I act as they were, as they never had me.

After studying my prey, figuring out how much and what I can get out of it; I try approaching it gently, as if I were to open a treasure chest without breaking it. I like when my vagina is tight under my fist strokes, and only loosens up slowly and gently to my cock.

In a way, the New World Order, other than its true political component, which is too complex for easy understanding by the masses, has grown in popularity just thanks to its conspiracy component. In fact, it may just resemble a Shakespearean drama.

As Shakespeare, through his plays, made culture available to the public of his time, which was greatly alliterate; so the New World Order has become popular among people, more because of its tragicomic reputation by mean of conspirators than politicians.

In a way, as renaissance began in England with the Elizabethan age and theater, right from the Globe Theatre in London; so the New World Order has been launched on the internet for the entire world arena to take a glimpse at its stories, themes and conspiracies.

Another conspiracy theory could be that the New World Order conspiracy itself was just the master plan of some more recent University Wits behind it all. At first, it may look like conspirators and New World Order opponents were winning the campaign.

However, the more time went by, the clearer it became that all the attacks onto the New World Order were just creating blowbacks at its very opponents. In way, in my opinion, that was the final proof that New World Order was just naturally meant to be.

One cannot oppose change when it is necessary for the survival of the human race and for the wellbeing of the whole planet. Almost everybody on the planet has now been exposed to the New World Order conspiracies; but the challenge is understanding its politics.

In fact, the political arena is not quite like drama in theaters or cinemas. Not only the risks and consequences are real, but one cannot even leave the room if what is being discussed is not of their liking. Now, this is the real face of the New World Order.

Perhaps I was just the University Wit behind the New World Order, or the cyber space master puppeteer who first depicted it as tragedy, then transformed it into comedy. Just like Shakespeare, I only aimed at becoming a shareholder of the Globe Theatre.

I am going to say it for the very last time. I was born in the ghetto, not in the city, just like Shakespeare. Without money one cannot leave the fucking ghetto, nor get enough pussy to satisfy his physical desires, and above anything else, won't enjoy a pension.

So, future generations; please do not blame me for having had to deal with age and sexual desires. I never wanted to be a hero like Garibaldi, but more of a pussy lover poet like Shakespeare. Despite I am not into tragedies at all, but prefer comedies instead.

Moreover, I can't really stand ghosts stories and the fear associated with death in general. To me, that's just way too much bullshit to waste my time with. I'd rather focus the time I have been granted in this life learning as much as I can before departing back.

Unfortunately though, I am not like Shakespeare. He was the man the right time, at the right place. In fact, he accomplished such great success thanks to great actors, able to deeply communicate with the audience, as well as great choreographers.

It is as if theater was in a way just waiting for Shakespeare to come take his part in it. I surely cannot say the same, as I am a lonely, loser fucking shoe strings poet. Truth being unless you are a genius like Shakespeare, you are not going to get out of the ghetto easily.

For instance, I don't know how to end this book either. Should the end be a tragedy or comedy? What mood do I want to leave my readers with, after finishing reading? How do I want to be remembered? These are the questions I am asking myself now.

My future has not been written yet, therefore it can go either way. However, only a woman can see both ways at the same time. A man, because of the missing leg in the one chromosome which makes him just that, may only see one way at the time; that's why.

Therefore, women may naturally like suspense, while men do not. Because I am not a woman, and I do not like suspense, nor I am gay, I'd like to end with a comedy. So, I wish for all my readers to just laugh at my unlucky existence, and that of my contemporaries.

After all, under many aspects, my life has been similar to that of Don Quixote, if not that I actually accomplished writing eight books after all my adventures and experiences. I guess, what I am trying to say is to look as a complete NATO, Western poet.

I have tried to fuse together all major previous literary works, productions and influences within the Romantic languages block as well as the Germanic and Celtic one. It will be difficult to get me without thinking from a NATO prospective of the Western world.

As I mean and feel the West, it is just like a flag held by a pole where Italy's the pole and California the farthest edge of the flag. That in a way is just the limit of the world as I really got to know it, with my own traveling experiences and intellectual closeness.

Under the light of what just said, claiming to be a New World Order poet is perhaps a bit too off-color. Nevertheless, it would be fair just saying I have been a NATO block poet, anticipating what art may look like in the New World Order and even behind.

Letteratura erotica italiana

Ars chiavatoria

A Venafro, per via d'Ovidio e della sua "Ars amatoria", non potevasi che esser ispirati dall'arte del chiavare.

Uomini e donne non sanno farne a meno, eppure li preti col voto di castità semper sembran il cazzo voler maniar.

Eppur nulla v'è de più semplice, o che un v'abbia la fica, oppure l'uccello. Due son li gusti, e per lo condimento, v'è pur la via dell'escremento.

La bocca l'han tutti, e non sol per mangiare, tant'è che l'è bel pur il succhiare. E v'è a chi piace pure il cane e l'asinello.

V'è chi sol una volta vuol provare, chi invece come ogni giorno vuol mangiare. V'è chi li vuol provar tutti li gusti, chi invece non ama variare.

V'è chi s'offre per arrotondare o insegnare, e a chi li figli va a cercare. V'è chi una pena vuol scampare, ed allora si da da fare.

V'è chi va con omo e donna, o l'omo con più donne e la donna con più omi. V'è chi s'incontra sol per scambiare, poi ognuno a casa vuol tornare.

Della malattia non a tutti sembra importare, e v'è chi lo fa proprio per infettare. V'è pur poi a chi invece piace sol guardare.

Con la pioggia e col sereno

Con la pioggia e col sereno, la vogliosa dell'uccello non può far meno.

Con la pioggia e col sereno, il rattuso dell'amante non può far meno.

Con la pioggia e col sereno, lesbica e ricchione sen leccar non san star.

Sega sega masto Ciccio, m'è venuta la verruca sul sasiccio.

Catechismo sessuale

Il gigolò e la mignotta fan dieci a botta.

A lo studente in cerca della prima occhiata, la mignotta può insegnar.

A la studentessa in cerca della prima maniata, il gigolò può insegnar.

Se allo studente, alla prima vista, la fessa non dovesse piacé, da un frocio deve farsi vedé.

Se alla studentessa, alla prima maniata, il cazzo non dovesse piacé, dalla monaca deve farsi vedé.

Se convento e seminario agli studenti non dovesse piacé, non v'è che intraprender lo mestié.

Vi sono poi i monogami prediletti, che a scambiar letti non son lieti né fatti. Alcune coppie fatte poi la monotonia evadon con altressì simil par, e non sol.

Però, sol al gigolò spetta l'arduo compito di un'aspirante madre a soddisfar, senza mai li figli a conoscer.

La "storta" di Venafro

Nell'osservare la Cattedrale di Venafro, si è notato che i massi riciclati da precedenti costruzioni romane potrebbero essere stati posizionati in maniera tutt'altro che causale o puramente strutturale. Infatti, notando quella che sembrerebbe essere la linea esterna delle fondamenta o base del duomo, dal lato di Villa Pilato, risalta l'utilizzo di pietre o fregi, generalmente posizionate a sostegno dei tetti dei templi greci e romani. Inoltre, su di esse poggiano i blocchi di pietra più grossi, quasi a reminiscenza dell'epoca cicoplica, tipici appunto dei templi. Di primo acchito, ciò sembrerebbe del tutto normale e logico, in quanto su di essi grava tutto il peso della struttura sovrastante, composta da blocchi più piccoli. Ad ogni modo, proprio in virtù della linea a fregi ondulati molto più sottile, tale ipotesi sembrerebbe senza senso, o i blocchi più grossi e pesanti sarebbero stati posizionati direttamente sulle fondamenta. Non solo questo, ma anche i due piloni sporgenti della parte inferiore del campanile hanno l'aspetto di due colonne rovesciate. Il senso logico di tale scelta potrebbe essere stato dettato dalla volontà specifica dei direttori dei lavori di voler celare un messaggio ben preciso, ossia quello di aver messo "sottosopra" i vecchi templi e la vecchia architettura, rovesciandone il contenuto a glorificazione del Cristo e della nuova religione. Anche il masso tondo sul quale poggia la colonna in granito un po' "storta" o inclinata, sembrerebbe essere una ruota di un antico frantoio con al centro l'incavo per l'asse che oggi ospita la colonna stessa. Dopotutto, Ponzio Pilato dimorava proprio sotto la Cattedrale e quella ruota potrebbe essere stata collocata in rimembranza delle parole di Cristo che su una tal pietra avrebbe fondato la propria Chiesa. D'altro canto, non a caso la facciata della chiesa di Santa Maria del Carmine risembla o richiama nello stile il Partenone e, subito dopo la storta, passando per la Cattedrale verso la chiesa di San Francesco, ci si incammina per la retta via, o rettifilo di Venafro. Questo, tutt'intorno al blocco di Villa Pilato.

Le chiese di Venafro

Sono rimasto colpito dalle chiese di Venafro ed in particolar modo dai campanili.

Ho vissuto un periodo di grave crisi economica, prima in America, poi purtroppo anche in Italia, ove sono giunto quando ancora la crisi stessa non veniva del tutto percepita.

A quattro anni dal mio rimpatrio e a due dal mio trasferimento a Venafro, la crisi si è presentata a tutti per ciò che veramente era, non solo quindi spirituale, ma anche come quanto già preannunciato.

Oggi è domenica 28/4/2013 ed il campanile dell'Annunziata ancora chiama le genti alla messa. A Venafro ho visto ciò che veramente era già accaduto a Davenport, sebbene con sembianze diverse.

Dapprima le campane mi hanno irritato, per via dell'intensificarsi dei rumori urbani, in quanto sovrapposte ai clacson irrispettosi dei divieti di segnalazioni acustiche urbane, all'intensificarsi del gracchiare delle cornacchie, del circolare di motorini con marmitte non omologate e dei camionisti menefreghisti.

Poi ho cominciato a realizzare che forse proprio solo le campane fossero l'unico richiamo di salvezza e d'aiuto a disposizione. I preti martellavano con le campane la popolazione affinché questa non cedesse alle segnalazioni che offrivano droga, prostituzione e quant'altro.

Tutti erano nel panico ed in cerca di qualche quattrino a qualsiasi costo e con qualsiasi mezzo. I preti d'altro canto con le loro campane incitavano la gente a partecipare alla vita cristiana, chiedendo ai più benestanti offerte per sfamare i meno fortunati.

Io stesso non ho esitato ad offrir loro il poco che avevo, invogliando mio padre ed altri a fare lo stesso.

Non nego che sia stato difficile convivere con i miei in questo periodo di crisi, in quanto le genti erano spaccate su chi dovesse o meritasse più aiuto.

I miei stessi parenti bestemmiavano e rifiutavano la Chiesa, pensando che forse satana, la mafia, il comunismo o la loro aggregazione al di fuori della chiesa potesse risolvere i problemi. C'era chi si ostinava a dire che la chiesa fosse ricca, ed io stesso debbo ammettere di averlo pensato e considerato, per tanto essa avrebbe dovuto svendere i propri beni per aiutare il prossimo.

Ad ogni modo, questi stessi personaggi, benché ricevessero pensioni o avessero un reddito fisso non facevano abbastanza per sfamare i più poveri, cui non rimaneva altro che rivolgersi alle organizzazioni cristiane per trovare non solo un conforto morale ma anche solo per un tozzo di pane.

In quel periodo, io stesso decisi di darmi alla strada, in cerca di un'evasione e di misericordia, trovando come unico e solo luogo di conforto alle scelleratezze da ma osservate, nei pressi della Cattedrale o Duomo di Venafro, ove scrissi queste poche righe a monito dei giorni presenti.

Dentro me infatti sapevo che solo la fede avrebbe potuto contribuire alla rinascita non solo del paese o della nazione, ma del mondo intero. Con Papa Francesco I, la Chiesa ha dato un segno importante ai propri fedeli ed il pastore può solo indicare la strada da percorrere al proprio gregge, che non essendo pecore ma esseri umani, dovrebbe essere in grado di capire che solo in chiesa c'è vera speranza per il futuro, tolleranza ed educazione di base o catechismo.

Troppi sono stati gli stereotipi negativi e maldicenze a circondare l'opera dei preti e delle suore, a tal punto che me stesso è stato molto difficile cercare la verità tra la baraonda o babilonia di calunnie che li circondavano.

Ho notato una certa incongruenza tra ciò che i fedeli facevano e dicevano. A volte proprio coloro che si mostravano più vicini al clero erano i primi a calunniarli fuori dalle chiese, creando quindi un velo di falsità e barriera per comprendere il vero messaggio dei pastori.

Confido però nel Papa Francesco I ed i parroci della Santa Chiesa Cattolica Romana nel riuscire a comunicare alle genti tutto il proprio sapere e le conoscenze minime necessarie a superare questo grave momento sociale ed economico.

Non posso che ammettere l'integrità della Chiesa, anche durante tutti gli altri gravi momenti storici, in quanto essa ha sempre cercato di tirar fuori l'umanità dalle tenebre in cui essa era precipitata, pur nei fatti spiacevoli come l'inquisizione e le indulgenze.

Ancor oggi infatti, è la Chiesa la vera magistra vitae, le cui chiese sono ancora i veri amori dei propri membri. Non ho dubbi che il rinnovamento della nuova società e della nuova umanità come sempre passerà dalla Chiesa, un'istituzione secolare e per tanto rigida e conservatrice.

Eppure, è proprio la sua rigidezza, disciplina e spirito di conservazione che le assicurano sempre un posto in prima fila nel futuro e non a caso la si definisce "Holy See" ossia "Santa Lungimiranza".

Campanili

Nell'osservare il campanile della Cattedrale di Venafro si sono notate decise similitudini col campanile delle Basiliche Paleocristiane di Cimitile. Le Basiliche di Cimitile vantano infatti il primato di ospitare il primo e più autentico campanile nella storia della cristianità. Sebbene a differenza del campanile del Duomo di Venafro, edificato in pietra, quello di Cimitile fu costruito in tufo, più abbondante nell'area del nolano, più malleabile e quindi più facilmente utilizzabile per le costruzioni. Sia Cimitile che Venafro erano territori sanniti già al tempo di Ponzio Pilato, sebbene ancora una volta Cimitile vanti di aver inventato la campana ed il suo utilizzo sul campanile.

Questo particolare è un ulteriore dettaglio a sostegno della tesi che il Cristianesimo si diffuse prima tra tutti proprio nel Sannio, per via di Ponzio Pilato al suo ritorno dalla Giudea. Ciò avvenne infatti prim'ancora che gli apostoli Paolo e Pietro intraprendessero il loro viaggio verso Roma e prim'ancora dunque della codificazione scritta dello stesso Cristianesimo, ossia la Sacra Bibbia.

Ciò implica che il Cristianesimo abbia sia una radice orale che scritta della propria dottrina, proprio come accadde precedentemente per l'Ebraismo, all'inizio tramandato oralmente, poi codificato per mezzo del Talmud.

Le due versioni quindi spiegherebbero le sottili differenze culturali esistenti tra le varie Chiese Cristiane, in particolare tra le popolazioni nordiche che furono esposte alla dottrina cristiana solo successivamente rispetto al meridione italiano, e certamente non per mano di Ponzio Pilato.

Questa distinzione la si può ancora trovare oggi negli ordinamenti giuridici degli anglosassoni ad esempio, rispetto all'Italia, che nel primo caso utilizzano il cosiddetto "Common Law", contrapposto al "Civil Law" o diritto civile.

Lo stesso discorso lo si può applicare alla sfera dei costumi sessuali che prima della caduta di Roma erano pressocché identici tra tutte le popolazioni pagane. Solo dopo la caduta di Roma ed il diffondersi in Europa della moralità giudaico-cristiana, ed il nascere delle lingue romanze si comincia a definire anche una diversità negli stili sessuali di queste popolazioni che, a detta di André Morali-Daninos, ne la "Storia della sessualità" è dovuta al fraintendimento del peccato originale come un vizio di natura sessuale anzicché come il peccato dell'uomo nel voler concorrere direttamente con Dio nella conoscenza celeste.

Ancora oggi, se tale contraddizione potesse essere risolta, la sessualità cernita dalla conoscenza del divino, rilegando quest'ultima al dominio degli uomini e donne di chiesa, e riservando il sesso a degli istruiti e preparati professionisti, allora una Chiesa veramente globale avrebbe ancora più possibilità di realizzarsi ed avvenire.

Ad ogni modo, resta il fatto che quasi sicuramente, da solo il Cristianesimo orale, come tramandato da Ponzio Pilato e dagli Apostoli, senza le successive codificazioni scritte, non sarebbe sopravvissuto sino ai giorni nostri.

Ciò è ad ulteriore conferma del mistero della fede, forse ancora troppo grande per essere completamente rivelato all'uomo moderno, in quanto non ancora in grado di recepirlo completamente o nella sua integrità, ma che solo attraverso il lavoro di più menti può far circolare il messaggio unitario, troppo grande per una sola mente.

Dopotutto il susseguirsi delle generazioni è la prova vivente di questo perpetuo cammino d'amore in continua evoluzione, ammesso che un vero traguardo mai si raggiungerà, o verrebbe meno l'infinità.

L'aspetto negativo o l'altro lato della medaglia è che questo processo purtroppo non è indolore, in quanto col passare del tempo e degli anni i più anziani sviluppano un certo risentimento verso i più giovani, un po' misto all'invidia ed al rigetto dei cambiamenti che gli si presentano via via sotto gli occhi.

Anche i campanili dopotutto invecchiano e le chiese si rinnovano con nuovi stili architettonici, ma non per questo vengon meno alla loro missione di guida e sprono verso quella luce che inesorabilmente di illumina e guida, sin dal Big Bang.

Architravi ad arco dell'anfitreato

Da un'analisi più attenta dell'anfiteatro romano di Venafro, allo stato attuale di conservazione al 2013, con tettoie ancora da riparare o provvisoriamente alloggiate in metallo, è possibile dedurre che esso sia stato un vero e proprio campo di gara tra diversi mastri muratori del luogo. Ogni edificio infatti è caratterizzato da un portone d'accesso composto da due colonne, generalmente in blocchi di pietra su cui poggia un architrave ad arco. Sembrerebbe che la gara o competizione dei masti fosse incentrata sulla costruzione del miglior arco, da cui i vari stili. È indubbio oggi notare quali fossero stati i migliori maestri degli architravi ad arco da loro realizzati in virtù del tempo trascorso e quali invece non altrettanto capaci.

La storia del salame milanese

Forse, più che dal latino o dall'osco, il napoletano deriva putroppo dall'arabo. Infatti, così narra la storia della salama milanese al femminile, o salame milanese al maschile, a seconda chi mangia.

C'era un giorno Mustafà che faceva il vu cumprà per le vie di Venafro. A un certo punto, una povera vecchiarella disse a Mustafà: "Ah salam t'ha vuò magnà?" E Mustafà rispose: "Eh!"

Quando la vecchietta gli da qualche fetta di salame milanese bello olioso olioso, perché faceva caldo e il salame era bello caldo, quindi olioso, Mustafà indietreggia e dice: "No no, oh salam no!"

La vecchietta non capendo dice a Mustafà se stesse parlando arabo. Ad ogni modo, Mustafà s'allontana gettando le fette di salame per la strada. La vecchietta pensa: "Vabbuò, c'pensan eh curnacchie."

Dopo un po' si sente il rombo di un motorino, poi un gran botto. La vecchietta s'affaccia e trova il motorino a terra e capisce che era scivolato sulle fette di salame che Mustafà aveva gettato.

Tutta dispiaciuta, la vecchietta può solo dire al malcapitao che le dispiace e che è tutta colpa di Mustafà che non s'era mangiato la salama milanese e che la conracchia non se n'era manco accorta.

Morale della favola, attenzione che sul salame milanese si scivola. Per gli italo americani poi il salame è una vera e propria maledizione, per via del nomignolo "grease balls," palle di lardo.

You should pray for a healthy mind in a healthy body. Ask for a stout heart that has no fear of death, and deems length of days the least of Nature's gifts that can endure any kind of toil, that knows neither wrath nor desire and thinks the woes and hard labors of Hercules better than the loves and banquets and downy cushions of Sardanapalus. What I commend to you, you can give to yourself; For assuredly, the only road to a life of peace is virtue.

orandum est ut sit mens sana in corpore sano. fortem posce animum mortis terrore carentem, qui spatium vitae extremum inter munera ponat naturae, qui ferre queat quoscumque labores, nesciat irasci, cupiat nihil et potiores Herculis aerumnas credat saevosque labores et venere et cenis et pluma Sardanapalli. monstro quod ipse tibi possis dare; semita certe tranquillae per virtutem patet unica vitae.

     –   Satire X; Roman poet Juvenal (10.356-64)